Earthquake Prepared

Securing Your Home
Protecting Your Family

by Joel Leach

Studio 4 Productions Publishing Company
Northridge, California
U.S.A.

Earthquake Prepared.
Copyright 1995 by Studio 4 Productions
Published by Studio 4 Productions
Post Office Box 280400
Northridge, CA 91328-0400

Library of Congress Catalog Card Number: 94-69682

International Standard Serial Number 1-882349-42-3

First Printing 1993
Second Printing 1994
Third Printing 1995 Revised Edition

Printed in the United States of America

TABLE OF CONTENTS

PREFACE

Those of us who live in earthquake country are repeatedly reminded to secure home furnishings against the eventuality of a major earthquake. However, prior to the publication of this book nobody had taken the time to describe in detail how to do it. Most of us homeowners aren't carpenters and we just aren't sure of what needs to be done and how best to accomplish the job. For instance:

- Is it okay to attach furniture directly to wallboard and, if so, what type of fastener is recommended?
- What are wall studs, how can I locate them and what type of fasteners is best for attaching to them?
- How should I secure my grandfather clock which has a very thin top piece?
- How can I best secure a wall unit which must stand 3 or 4 inches from the wall?
- When I attach a bookcase to the wall, how can I hide the brackets from view?
- Is there any way to keep valuable pictures and art work from being shaken from their hooks during an earthquake?
- What can I use to secure my computer and other expensive office equipment?
- What's the best way to secure my water heater?
- How can I keep kitchen cabinet doors from bouncing open and dumping breakable dishware and food items during a strong earthquake?
- Are there special precautions which I should take to make my garage safer?
- Is there anything I can do to minimize the chance of having my glass patio doors shatter during a jarring quake?
- How can I minimize the risk of having my house shaken from its foundation during a strong earthquake?
- Is earthquake insurance a good investment and how much does it cost?
- What food items should I store and how much of each per family member?
- How much water should I store and how often must it be rotated?
- What are the special needs of the disabled, and how can they be addressed?
- Mobile home communities aren't like single family residences. What are their special needs and what must their residents do to be prepared?
- Apartment residents are to a great extent dependent on their neighbors. What special steps should be taken in advance of a major earthquake?
- Condo & townhome residents have unique insurance risks. Can they be minimized?
- In the event we exhaust our stored water, what other sources of water might be available in our home?
- What's the simplest way to sterilize water?
- Is it okay to drink pool water?
- If all gas service is shut off, how can we heat food for our baby?
- What basics should a medical kit contain?
- In the event the sewer system is not operating, how should we deal with human waste?

Although the author and the publisher hope that none of us will ever have to deal with The Big One, we must face the reality that there is a considerable likelihood that we will at some time experience a severe and damaging earthquake. If and when that happens, we hope you and your family will survive it without harm or loss. We also hope this book will have helped you do so.

Acknowledgments

Dozens of experts and agencies contributed to this book, including architects, structural engineers, contractors, medical personnel, utility personnel, hardware store personnel, insurance companies, manufacturers, authors, video producers, corporations, associations and installers. For this assistance, the author is most grateful.

Special words of thanks go to the following individuals who willingly made themselves and their considerable knowledge available without hesitation: Dr. Frannie Winslow (Office of Emergency Services), Katherine Firpo, Research Assistant at the Bay Area Regional Earthquake Preparedness Project, Arnold Bookbinder (Structural Engineer), David Helfant (Structural Engineer), Doug Silver (Structural Engineer), Mark Joslin (Q Safety), Stan Argent (Pro-Motion Ltd.), Karen Ervin-Pershing, Leonard Nelson, Roberta Pigner.

Artists: Kimberly Blake Kilgore and Greg McKinney

Important Notice

At this point in time, science cannot yet accurately predict when or where earthquakes will occur. Even if earthquakes could be predicted, it would be virtually impossible to anticipate the forces and earth movement which would result.

Factors such as the type of earthquake, the depth of its epicenter, one's proximity to the event, soil type and, of course, its intensity cause us to realize that all we can do is our best as we attempt to prepare for what's often considered to be nature's most potentially devastating natural occurrence.

This book has been written to help guide the average homeowner through the processes involved in securing one's home and family in anticipation of a major earthquake. Although the information contained in this book has been obtained from and verified by experts in a variety of fields, the accuracy thereof cannot be guaranteed. Neither the author nor the publishing company assumes any responsibility regarding the information, the products listed herein or the application thereof.

Readers are urged to consult with engineers, contractors, medical authorities, utility personnel, insurance agents and any and all other appropriate authorities and experts to learn as much as possible about earthquake preparedness. A number of such sources are listed in the final chapter of this book. Others may be located in the yellow pages of your local telephone directory.

The publisher does not assume and hereby disclaims any liability to any party for any loss or damage caused by errors and omissions, whether such errors result from negligence, accident or any other cause.

Unlike other earth traumas such as tornadoes, hurricanes, floods, etc., earthquakes strike unexpectedly. And, they vary tremendously in intensity from those which rattle dishes to those which do massive destruction.

In a major earthquake, you may experience shaking which will start off gently and, within a few seconds, grow to such intensity it will knock you off your feet. Another time, an earthquake will consist of a sudden jolt. Regardless of the type, you and your family will have only a few seconds to react. The best way to protect yourself and your family is to be prepared.

HOW EARTHQUAKES ARE MEASURED

The vibrations produced by earthquakes are measured by *seismographs* which transcribe an earthquake's motion into zig-zag lines called a *seismogram.* From the data recorded in a seismogram, the time, epicenter and depth of an earthquake can be determined and an estimate can be made of its relative size and the amount of energy that was released.

The point on a fault beneath the earth's surface where a rupture begins is called the *focus* or *hypocenter* of the earthquake. The point on the earth's surface directly above the hypocenter is called the *epicenter.*

Two Scales for Measuring Earthquakes: Magnitude & Intensity

The Richter Magnitude Scale

The *Richter Scale* measures the *magnitude* of an earthquake. This scale uses whole numbers and decimals. It's important to realize that magnitude varies logarithmically with the wave amplitude of a quake. That means that each whole number step of magnitude on the scale represents an increase of ten times in the measured wave amplitude of an earthquake. Therefore, the amplitude of an 8.3 magnitude earthquake is not twice as large as a shock of magnitude 4.3 but *10,000* times as large.

Richter magnitude can also provide an estimate of the amount of energy released during an earthquake. For every unit increase in magnitude, there is about a 31-fold increase in energy. That means an 8.3 earthquake releases almost *one million* times more energy than an earthquake of magnitude 4.3

Relationship between Earthquake Magnitude and Energy

The volumes of the spheres at right are roughly proportional to the amount of energy released by earthquakes of the magnitudes given, and illustrate the exponential relationship between magnitude and energy. At the same scale, the energy released by the San Francisco earthquake of 1906 (Richter magnitude 8.3) would be represented by a sphere with a *radius* of 110 feet.

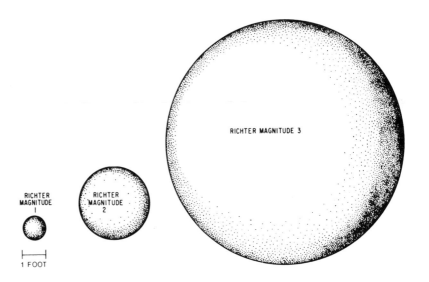

The Modified Mercalli (MM) Intensity Scale

The *Modified Mercalli intensity scale* expresses an earthquake's *intensity.* This is a subjective measure which depends on the effects of a quake such as damage at a particular location. Although there is only one [Richter] magnitude number for a given earthquake there may well be several values of [MM] intensity.

The MM intensity scale is perhaps more meaningful to the layman because it is based on actual observations of an earthquake's effects at specific places. Because the data used for assigning MM intensities is obtained only from firsthand reports, it sometimes takes weeks or even months before an intensity map can be assembled following an earthquake.

On the Modified Mercalli intensity scale, values range from I to XII. While an earthquake has only one [Richter] magnitude, it can have many intensities, which decrease with distance from the epicenter.

The MM Scale Descriptions

I Not felt except by a very few under especially favorable circumstances.

II Felt only by a few persons at rest, especially on upper floors of buildings. Delicately suspended objects may swing.

III Felt quite noticeably indoors, especially on upper floors of buildings, but many people do not recognize it as an earthquake. Standing motorcars may rock slightly. Vibration like passing of a truck. Duration estimated.

IV During the day felt indoors by many, outdoors by few. At night some awakened. Dishes, windows, doors disturbed; walls make cracking sound. Sensation like heavy truck striking building. Standing motor cars rocked noticeably.

V Felt by nearly everyone, many awakened. Some dishes, windows, etc. broken; a few instances of cracked plaster; unstable objects overturned. Disturbances of trees, poles, and other tall objects sometimes noticed. Pendulum clocks may stop.

VI Felt by all, many frightened and run outdoors. Some heavy furniture moved; a few instances of fallen plaster or damaged chimneys. Damage slight.

VII Everybody runs outdoors. Damage negligible in building of good design and construction; slight to moderate in well-built ordinary structures; considerable in poorly built or badly designed structures; some chimneys broken. Noticed by persons driving motor cars.

VIII Damage slight in specially designed structures; considerable in ordinary substantial buildings, with partial collapse; great in poorly built structures. Panel walls thrown out of frame structures. Fall of chimneys, factory stacks, columns, monuments, walls. Heavy furniture overturned. Sand and mud ejected in small amounts. Changes in well water. Persons driving motor cars disturbed.

IX Damage considerable in specially designed structures; well-designed frame structures thrown out of plumb; great in substantial buildings, with partial collapse. Buildings shifted off foundations. Ground cracked conspicuously. Underground pipes broken.

X Some well-built wooden structures destroyed; most masonry and frame structures destroyed with foundations; ground badly cracked. Rails bent. Landslides considerable from river banks and steep slopes. Shifted sand and mud. Water splashed (slopped) over banks.

XI Few, if any, (masonry) structures remain standing. Bridges destroyed. Broad fissures in ground. Underground pipelines completely out of service. Earth slumps and land slips in soft ground. Rails bend greatly.

XII Damage total. Practically all works of construction are damaged greatly or destroyed. Waves seen on ground surface. Lines of sight and level are destroyed. Objects are thrown upward into the air.

Comparison of Richter Magnitude and Modified Mercalli Intensity

Richter	MM	Expected MM Maximum Intensity (at Epicenter)
2	I-II	Usually detected only by instruments
3	III	Felt indoors
4	IV-V	Felt by most people; slight damage
5	VI-VII	Felt by all; many frightened and run outdoors; damage minor to moderate
6	VII-VIII	Everybody runs outdoors; damage moderate to major
7	IX-X	Major damage
8+	X-XII	Total and major damages

The Ten Largest Earthquakes in the Contiguous United States

Mag.	Date	Location
8.25	April 18, 1906	San Francisco, California
8.2	February 7, 1812	New Madrid, Missouri
8.0	December 16, 1811	New Madrid, Missouri
7.9	January 9, 1857	Fort Tejon, California
7.8	January 23, 1812	New Madrid, Missouri
7.8	March 26, 1872	Owens Valley, California
7.8	October 3, 1915	Pleasant Valley, Nevada
7.8	July 21, 1952	Kern County, California
7.7	August 31, 1866	Charleston, South Carolina
7.6	December 16, 1811	New Madrid, Missouri

Earthquakes and Bombs

A more graphic—albeit more sinister—way to demonstrate the tremendous amount of energy expended by earthquakes is to compare them with mankind's own deadly forces of destruction: bombs.

An earthquake reading of 5.0 on the Richter scale is equal to **a 50-megaton atom bomb**

An earthquake reading of 6.0 on the Richter scale is equal to ***one hundred* 50-megaton atom bombs**

An earthquake reading of 7.0 on the Richter scale is equal to ***ten thousand* 50-megaton atom bombs**

An earthquake reading of 8.0 on the Richter scale is equal to ***one million 50-megaton* atom bombs**

An earthquake reading of 9.0 on the Richter scale is equal to ***one hundred million* 50-megaton atom bombs**

An earthquake reading of 10.0 on the Richter scale is equal to ***one billion* 50-megaton atom bombs**

California is expecting an earthquake of 8.0 or more to strike anytime within the next 30 years. It *might* happen tomorrow.

Note: Information and artwork regarding Richter & Mercalli Scales was drawn from Publication DMG NOTE 32 by the California Department of Conservation Division of Mines and Geology

HARDWARE & SPECIAL PRODUCTS

To Be Used In Securing Your Home

This chapter will introduce you to a variety of hardware-type items which will make it possible for you to secure virtually all valuable property in your home. While some of the items shown here are probably already known to you, it's likely you'll encounter new applications of these products—so you just might want to skim through everything at least lightly.

In this chapter, you'll also learn about newly developed and relatively unknown products which will enable you to secure valuable pictures, artwork, computers and glassware—things which were never before able to be protected against the violence of an earthquake.

Because not all of us qualify as handymen, we'll start with what may seem to some to be elementary information. If you're up to speed on basics such as screws and bolts, feel free to jump ahead to the items with which you're less familiar.

###

There are three types of common fasteners: nails, screws and bolts Nails are minimally effective when attempting to stabilize in the event of an earthquake. So let's forget about nails.

Screws

Screws are fine if you're sure the screw will be able to dig deeply into something *solid* like a wall stud. (Note: Screws are no good if you must attach to something *hollow* like wall board. See next section for instructions dealing with attaching to wall board.)

A screw offers far more gripping power than a nail. Furthermore, a screw may be easily removed with minimal damage when the time comes to detach the furniture from the wall. Screws are installed with a screwdriver.

Screws are available in a variety of types. Those which are most likely to serve your purposes in securing your property against the damage of earthquakes are shown here.

Flathead screws are used whenever the screw's head must be flush with the surface. Available with both slotted and cross-slot type heads.

Phillips head screws are designed to minimize screwdriver slippage. A Phillips screwdriver is required.

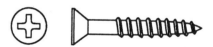

Oval head screws must be partially countersunk. They look better than flathead screws.

Roundhead screws are used where countersinking is not possible because the fastened piece is too thin. They may also be used when a washer is required.

Lag screws (also called lag bolts are just heavy-duty screws with square heads. They are installed with a wrench rather than a screwdriver.

Screw Sizes

Screw sizes are designated by both length and diameter. The length is designated in inches, up to a maximum of 6 inches. Always select screw lengths so that at least *two-thirds* of the screw length passes into the material to which you are fastening.

The diameter of a screw is measured by a *gauge number* starting with 2 and continuing up to 16.

Installing Screws

Always first drill a hole **smaller than the screw's diameter** into the wood. This not only enables the screw to be installed with considerably less effort, but also prevents the wood from splitting.

Screw Washers

Washers are often used under screw heads to gain added bearing surface. Be certain to match washer to the screw's diameter and head-type.

Bolts

A bolt is a two-piece fastener: the bolt and a nut used for tightening. (In the case of toggle bolts and molly bolts, the nuts are replaced by devices which open or expand inside the wall as the bolt is turned.)

There are several types of bolts (ex.: machine bolts, carriage bolts, stove bolts, turn-buckle bolts, etc.) which have not been included here because they are not intended for uses included in this book.

The two most useful bolt types in earthquake damage prevention are the toggle bolt and the molly bolt. ***Please note: Neither toggle bolts nor molly bolts should ever be used to secure heavy pieces of furniture. Use bolts which go directly into wall studs for such jobs.***

Toggle bolts are used when fastening to hollow walls. First, drill a hole large enough to pass the spring-loaded wings through. The wings will open and bear against the inside of the wall as the screw's head is turned.

Pass screw through the fixture then re-install it in wing-like base. Close arms and push entire bolt through hole in wall.

Once inside wall, the bolt's wings will spring open. Next, pull on fixture so that wings grip inside of wall.

Tighten bolt until firmly seated.

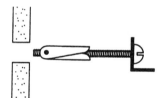
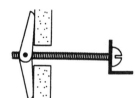
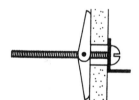

Molly bolts, similar to toggle bolts, are also used for attaching to hollow walls. Like the toggle bolt, the molly bolt is passed through a pre-drilled hole. As the head is turned, the legs expand to grip against the wall's inner surface.

Pass molly bolt through pre-drilled hole in wall.

Tighten until pressure is felt, then stop and remove bolt.

Pass bolt through the fixture, then re-install it and tighten until firmly seated.

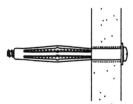
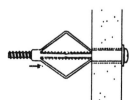
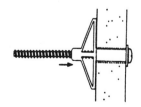

Masonry bolts are used to attach heavy objects (ex. water heaters) to masonry walls.

Drill a hole just wide enough for anchor to fit snugly. Be certain to drill deeply enough for anchor to fit.

Pass bolt through the fixture, then screw it into anchor.

Tighten bolt to expand anchor and firmly seat fixture.

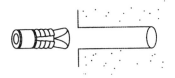 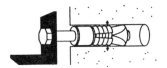 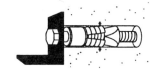

Miscellaneous Items

Screw eyes can support substantial loads if they are screwed into wall studs. They support lighter loads when screwed only into wallboard. The closed loop keeps wires and hooks securely attached. (Note: Screw eyes are ultra-secure picture hangers. First install the screw hanger in the wall, then run hanger wire *through* the eye.)

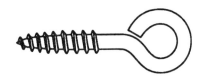

Screw hooks like screw eyes, can support substantial loads if screwed directly into wall studs. The advantage to screw hooks over screw eyes is that their design allows for loads to be easily lifted and disengaged from them. That advantage can become a distinct disadvantage in an earthquake, when things tend to bounce about.

Gate hooks and **snap hooks** (with swivels) are made with spring-loaded clasps to prevent them from disengaging. Gate hooks of this type are excellent for securing large items which must be removed on occasion.

 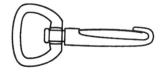

Earthquake-Safe Picture Fasteners *(Q-Safety Products)* are attached to the wall with a nail just like conventional picture hangers. There the similarity ends. These unique Picture Fasteners offer a snap-shut design which prevents pictures from leaping off the hooks during violent earthquake-type shaking. When pulled, the dangling string opens the fastener for easy picture removal. Small Velcro® pads, are supplied with the fasteners. They keep the picture from swinging and banging against the wall and shattering the glass.

Pull to
release
picture

Corner braces (corner irons) are excellent for attaching furniture to the wall when furniture either touches or stands close to the wall. Use multiple corner braces on wide pieces of furniture. They are available in a variety of sizes as shown here.

Use screws to attach the corner brace to the wall if you're able to screw directly into wall studs. Use toggle bolts or molly bolts if you must secure the furniture to wallboard.

For attaching corner brace to the furniture piece, use the longest wood screws possible (without passing all the way through the piece). (An even better choice would be small bolts which pass all the way through the wood and are secured on the inside with nuts. Of course, this works only if the bolt will not be visible.)

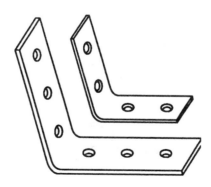

"T" Straps and **"L" Straps** are metal pieces which are installed using either nails or screws, although screws obviously hold better. "T" and "L" straps (plus many other shapes to suit a multitude of applications) are highly recommended for strengthening major wood joints. Both because of their size and the fact that they are unfinished, they are not generally used in a home's living area where they may be seen. They are best suited for use in the garage where they will add considerable strength and stability to shelving.

Plumber's tape isn't "tape" in the conventional sense. It's a 5/8" wide strip of flexible metal several feet in length which has holes drilled through it every half inch. Plumber's tape can be cut to any length and secured just like a "T" or "L" strap, using screws or bolts.

Plumber's tape offers two significant advantages: the fact that it can be custom-cut to fit the length needed and that it's flexible and can be easily bent and shaped to fit any job.

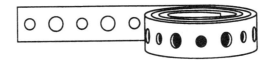

Q-Safety, Quake Hold! and *WorkSafe Technologies™* all manufacture items designed to secure bookshelf items. They consist of elastic cords with buckles or latches at the ends which attach to a bookcase's side pieces. The cord's elasticity allows for items to be taken easily from the shelf.

The **Super Strap™** *(Q-Safety Products)* and the **Furniture Strap** *(Quake Hold!)* are heavy-duty straps with pre-cut, grommetted holes designed to be used for securing bookcases and other large furniture units to walls. *Quake Hold!* markets a **Big Screen & Appliance Strap** as well.

Wire is available in a variety of thicknesses at any hardware store. It is also available as single-strand or multiple (braided) strands. Braided wire is more durable.

Fishing line which is nearly invisible, may also be used for securing items such as priceless vases. First, run the wire around the vase's neck, then pass it through a screw eye which has been installed either in the shelf or in the wall behind it.

Latches

Cabinet latches are inexpensive plastic devices designed to keep children away from knives, cleaning supplies and other dangerous household items. However, they are capable of not only keeping little people *out* but also of keeping objects *in* during an earthquake.

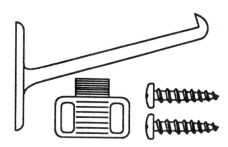

Positive Latches (sometimes called Touch Latches or Push Latches) are sophisticated mechanisms which use spring-loaded hooks to keep cabinet doors closed. Apply slight pressure to the outside of the door to disengage the lock.

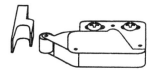

Window Film

Safety & Security Film, a heavy duty reflective film designed to make windows break-resistant, is designed to hold glass in place even when it is broken, an important consideration, given the violent shaking which results during most earthquakes. S & S Film also protects furniture and carpeting from the sun's harmful rays. It costs only slightly more than the non-break-resistant films available in hardware stores.

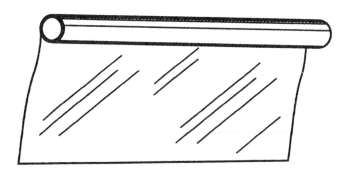

Adhesive-Type Items

Silicone Adhesive comes in a squeeze tube and may be applied to virtually any surface, including glass, ceramics, metal, wood, wallboard, etc. Available in "clear", it dries rapidly and offers a strong bond which works well, for instance, for stabilizing pictures on their hooks. Silicone adhesive is easily removed.

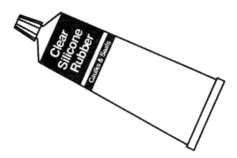

Velcro®, a unique two-part fastener with one part consisting of hooks and the other of loops, is available as a tape with self-stick adhesive on the reverse sides. It's ideal for securing and stabilizing light objects. When applied to the bottom of a hanging picture, Velcro not only keeps the picture from tilting but also minimizes the risk of the picture "jumping" from its hook during an earthquake.

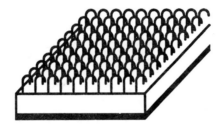

VersaGRIP™ *(Q-Safety Products)* is a type of industrial-strength Velcro® which uses a "T" hook rather than a "J" hook for increased gripping power. Developed for securing heavy items such as computers, hard disk drives, printers, typewriters, music keyboards, VCRs, stereo equipment, etc., VersaGRIP™ also uses a high strength adhesive.

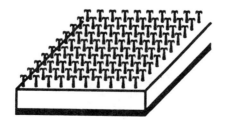

VersaBLOCK™ *(Q-Safety Products)* and **Fastener Blocks** *(Quake Hold!)* are, for all practical purposes, newly designed and improved industrial-strength Velcro designed to hold small electronics and appliances. Available in a variety of sizes.

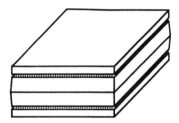

Quake Hold!™ *(Trevco)* and **Quake Wax™** *(Conservation Materials, Ltd.™)* are putty-like substances which are applied to the bottom of objects made of glass, crystal, china, figurines, etc. Next, the object is pressed downward on a shelf. They help keep valuable items from jumping from their shelves during earthquakes. Both are removable and reusable and claim they will not harm fine finishes.

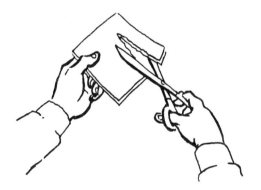

Specialty Items For Securing Electronics

VersaBRACE™ *(Q-Safety Products)* is a flexible, high-strength nylon device which may be bent to fit nearly any desired shape. Particularly suited for securing computers and other electronic equipment. Available in 2" and 3" sizes.

VersaTETHER™ *(Q-Safety Products)* is a device which secures items such as keyboards, monitors and telephones, while allowing the user to move them to a comfortable work position. Available in several sizes.

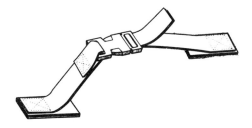

Thumb Lock, Quake Hold! and WorkSafe Technologies all manufacture straps in a variety of lengths with quick-release fasteners at both ends. With a little creative thinking, the device can be used to fasten objects which would seemingly defy security measures.

QuakeMat *(WorkSafe Technologies™)* is a product designed for securing computers, typewriters and similar items. Made of a high-density material, it grips both the equipment's feet and the desktop surface to limit movement.

WHAT YOU NEED TO KNOW ABOUT WALLS BEFORE STARTING

Without question, your furniture will be most secure if you attach it to a wall stud. A stud is a vertical wooden beam in the frame of a building (inside the walls) to which other boards and sheathing (wallboard) are attached. Studs are generally 2 x 4's spaced 16 inches apart.

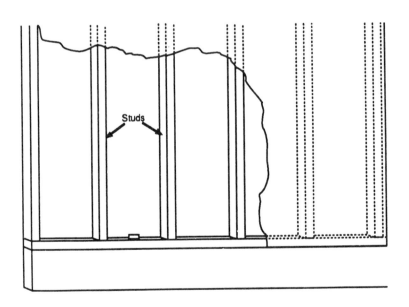

Locating a Wall Stud

You'll want to find out if there's a wall stud located where you need it behind the furniture you want to secure. There are several methods for doing this.

1)   **Stud finder:** An inexpensive magnetic stud finder (shown below) is available at hardware stores for about $5. Just slide the stud finder along the baseboard where

its magnet will detect nails which were used to attach the baseboard to a wall stud. Then follow an imaginary line straight up the wall from there and you can be sure you're attaching to a stud. Better: try an *electronic* stud finder—they rely on density changes. Both types used in combination might be best of all.

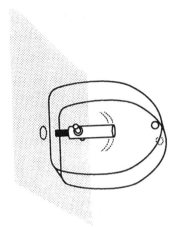

2)   **Tap the wall** lightly (the butt end of a screwdriver works well) at points above nails which may be visible in the baseboard. A hollow sound means there is no stud. A solid sound indicates the presence of a stud. To be sure you've found a stud, use a small drill (1/8 inch) to bore holes in the wall slightly above the baseboard. Drill several holes side by side until you bore into the stud. Then follow an imaginary line straight up the wall from there and you can be sure you're attaching to a stud.

3)   **Baseboard removal:** With the baseboard off, check to see where two panels of drywall meet. This point will indicate the center of a stud. This method also works with paneled walls. Then follow an imaginary line straight up the wall from there and you can be sure you're attaching to a stud.

4)   **Measuring from the corner:** Studs are generally located either 12 or 16 inches apart, depending on building codes in a particular area. Try measuring out from the corner of a room to find the approximate location of a stud, then use the drilling technique described above to find the exact stud location.

If There's No Stud Just Where You Need It

There will be times when you'll find that there's no wall stud centered where you need it behind your stereo system or grandfather clock, so you'll have to attach it to the wallboard. Although wallboard isn't as stable as a stud, it should suffice, providing you select an appropriate fastener.

LET'S GET STARTED!

The Water Heater

Because of their tall, thin design, water heaters are inherently unstable in earthquake country. If the water heater moves or topples, it will likely break the water and gas lines, depleting a much-needed source of water and possibly causing a fire. Whereas homeowners were once advised to buy some plumber's tape and a few lag bolts to do the job themselves, recent research has shown that the job is best accomplished when the water heater is braced in a variety of ways using an array of nuts, bolts, shelf brackets, wood 2 x 4's and plumbers tape. But for the not-so-handyperson, even the thought of assembling the items might prove to be too much!

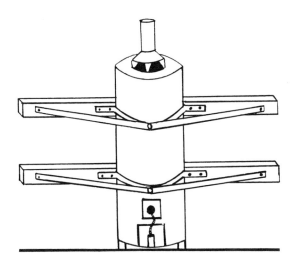

Not to worry. You can now buy kits at most home improvement centers which contain detailed instructions along with all the pieces needed to do the job!

It's understandable, however, if you'd prefer hiring an expert to do the job and fortunately such experts *are* available in many areas. It's suggested that you begin by contacting your local gas company to find out if they will do the strapping job for you. After all, they're experts on the topic.

If you wish, you can instead hire a licensed plumbing contractor—but it is still strongly suggested that you contact your local gas company to obtain printed information (diagrams, instructions, etc.) which tell how the gas company feels the job is best accomplished. Then make sure the contractor you hire will do the job to those specifications.

Note: Laws in some areas demand that water heaters which are located in garages be raised a minimum of 18 inches above the floor. This is because fumes from spilled flammables hover close to the garage floor where they could be easily ignited by the water heater's pilot light. Metal water heater stands which solve that problem are now available at many hardware stores. (Note: Some plumbers might secure your garage water heater without advising you that to do the job without elevating it 18 inches is against the law in your area. Obviously, this is not recommended.)

Tall Furniture With a *Thick* Top Piece of Solid Wood, Which Stands Close to The Wall

Anchor bookcases and other tall or top-heavy furniture to the wall using corner braces or straps of the type made by Q-Safety or Quake Hold! To make both corner braces and straps less noticeable, you might consider inverting them, as shown, so they are hidden by the furniture itself. (This procedure requires marking the furniture's height, moving it away from the wall to attach the brace or strap, then returning the furniture and screwing (or bolting) the hardware to it.) Note: exceptionally wide pieces of furniture may require two or even three such devices.

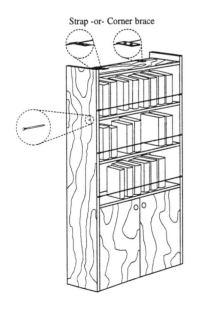

Strap -or- Corner brace

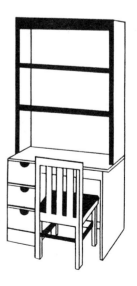

Tall Furniture With a *Thin* Top Piece
Which Must Stand Away From The Wall

Grandfather clocks, for instance, often fall into this category. Attaching a corner brace or Super Strap to the top board of a piece of furniture which may be only 1/4 inch thick will serve no purpose.

In cases such as this, measure and cut a piece of plumber's tape long enough to reach from the wall all the way to the back side of the clock's front-piece where the wood is much thicker. Next, attach the plumber's tape to the wall using a lag bolt, molly bolt or toggle bolt. Then, use at least *two screws* to attach the other end to the clock's facade.

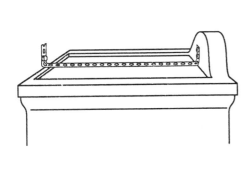
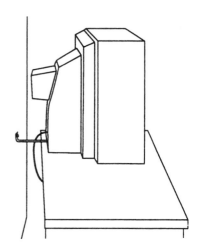

Securing Bookcases and Their Contents

Bookcases often contain shelves which sit on adjustable metal pegs. During earthquakes, shelves of this type sometimes bounce off the pegs, dumping the books on the floor.

To prevent this from happening, drive small finishing nails (called "brads") through the side of the bookcase, and into the shelf itself. Next, countersink the nails slightly and cover the holes with woodworker's colored pencils (available at hardware stores).

Even if the shelves stay in place, books often "walk" off the shelves. A bungee-type cord with special fasteners at each end solves this problem quite handily. It is available from both Q-Safety and Quake Hold!

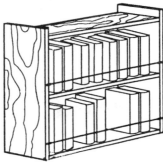

Crystal, Ceramics, Glassware and Art Objects

Quake Hold!™ is a malleable, putty-like substance designed for securing figurines, crystal, collectibles, heirlooms, knick-knacks, statues, plate holders, glass, vases, antiques, etc. It will adhere to wood, tile, tables, shelves, cabinets and various other surfaces. A little daub is applied to the bottom of an object before it is placed on a shelf. And, it's reusable.

The manufacturers of *Quake Hold!™* also point out that it's usable on certain items up to 30 lbs. in weight. That would include items such as a 13 in. TV.

A little-known but effective trick used by museums which must protect priceless items of art: the object is encircled at its thinnest spot by fine nylon string (similar to that used by fishermen). Then the string's ends are secured out of sight. Obviously, this works best with display-type items—not items like crystalware which must be removed to be used.

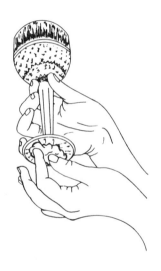

Pictures and Hanging Artwork

Pictures and hanging art work often leap from their hooks during strong earthquakes. People have sought solutions to this damaging and potentially costly problem for years.

Forget crimping conventional hooks shut. And forget about using screw eyes—it's too hard detaching the wire from the picture, threading it through the screw eye and then trying to put it all together again in the limited space behind the picture.

Q-Safety's *Earthquake Safe Picture Fasteners* offer a far better solution. Attached to the wall with a nail, these unique picture fasteners offer a snap-shut design which prevents the picture from leaping off its wall hook. (The dangling string, when pulled, opens the fastener for easy picture removal.) Small Velcro® pads, also enclosed, keep the picture from swinging and banging against the wall and shattering the glass.

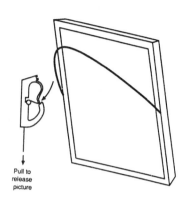

Pull to
release
picture

Cabinet Doors

Cabinets, particularly kitchen cabinets, contain numerous breakable items. Not only do you want to avoid loss of food during a period when supermarkets might well be closed, but you also don't want to have broken glass strewn all over the floor which you'll not be able to vacuum up—because you'll probably not have electricity for a while either.

Cabinets (and drawers) can be secured with Positive Latches (often called Mechanical Latches) The inexpensive child-proof type allow a cabinet door to open just enough to allow one's fingers to reach in and release it.

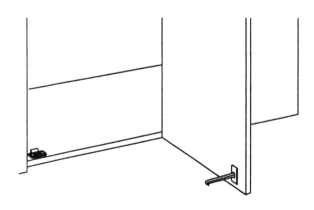

Positive Latches are an alternative to the simple child-proof latches. Made of metal, these latches generally contain a mechanism which utilizes a spring-loaded catch and a roller device to hold a cabinet door shut. One *pushes* against the cabinet door to release a Positive Latch.

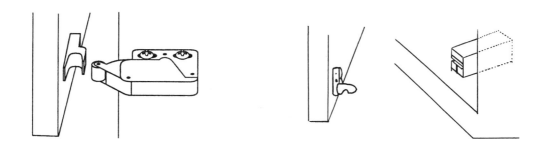

Attaching Computers, Stereo Components, VCRs, Televisions, Microwaves, Table Lamps, Clocks, Etc.

Method #1:

Attach valuable and/or heavy (and therefore potentially dangerous) electronics to their shelves so they won't bounce off and smash on the floor. Velcro, with its two sticky pads and interlocking hook-and-loop design, works quite well for low-profile, relatively lightweight items.

However, Velcro's moderate-strength grip may not be sufficient to secure taller, heavier units such as computers, microwaves and table lamps. For such special applications, Q-Safety and Quake Hold! have designed an "industrial strength" grippers using a different hook design which offers considerably more gripping power.

These products, available in pre-cut blocks of various sizes, are installed like Velcro. Also like Velcro, they can be pulled apart and re-engaged as the need arises.

A **QuakeMat** *(WorkSafe Technologies™)* grips both the equipment's feet and the desktop surface to limit movement. It is installed without adhesive by merely placing it beneath the equipment item. It will not damage wood surfaces and it can be easily moved to a new location.

Attaching Computers, Stereo Components, VCRs, Televisions, Microwaves, Etc.

Method #2:
It's important to consider the height-to-base-area-ratio of the equipment to be fastened. The taller something is, relative to the area of its base, the more likely it will topple in an earthquake.

Also, it's sometimes necessary to stack one piece of equipment on top of another, a common practice with computers which sit on top of their hard disk drives. For that reason, Q-Safety invented VersaBRACE™ fasteners. Available in a number of sizes, these flexible devices are easily bent into virtually any shape. Their "feet" have the VersaGRIP fasteners on them which can be easily disengaged if it's necessary to move a piece of equipment.

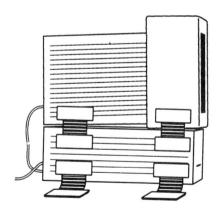

Method #3:
Another design approach capitalizes on a unique flip-type of lock which makes it possible to disengage equipment instantaneously. This type of strap, available from a variety of manufacturers, can use multiple buckles as shown.

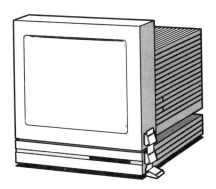

Big-Screen TVs, Appliances And Other Large Furniture

Quake Hold! has introduced a strap designed specifically to protect items such as big-screen TV's, refrigerators, stoves, washers and dryers, fish tanks, pianos and other large furniture pieces. They are designed to look good while allowing easy removal for cleaning and servicing.

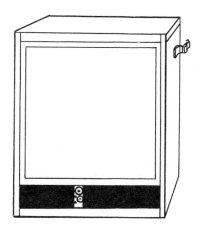

Large Windows and Patio Doors

Eliminate both costly replacement and potential hazard to you and your family by having safety film installed on large windows and glass patio doors. It is available clear or tinted in a variety of shades.

Applied to the inside surface of the glass, it not only adds strength, but also tends to hold shattered glass in place. Similar to, but much heavier than its lighter weight cousin available at most hardware stores, safety and security film offers the same relief from the sun, the same security factors *plus* the added strength. Plus, it's only slightly higher in price.

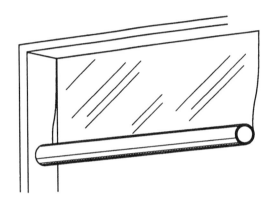

In the Garage

Many of us store large items in the garage rafters–items likely to be shaken loose and dropped on our automobile! If you feel you must store wood, model train boards, and various other items in your garage rafters, you're urged to use clothesline to tie them securely in place.

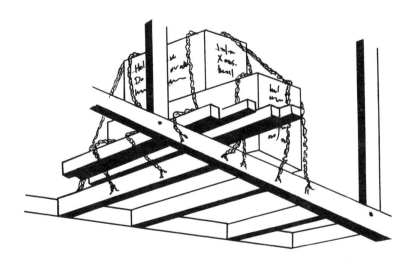

Store all liquids and all breakable containers on the garage floor. Keep only those flammable items which are essential and are used regularly; dispose of all others in accordance with city ordinances. Make sure they are in metal rather than glass containers and store them well away from the water heater or any other heat or electrical source.

It's wise to stretch a piece of wire or bungee-type cord across the fronts of shelves to hold items in place during an earthquake. Even better: also add a short board on the front of the shelf, sticking up "lip style", to keep items from falling beneath the wire.

Store all paint cans directly on the garage floor—never on shelves where they might be knocked off during a strong earthquake.

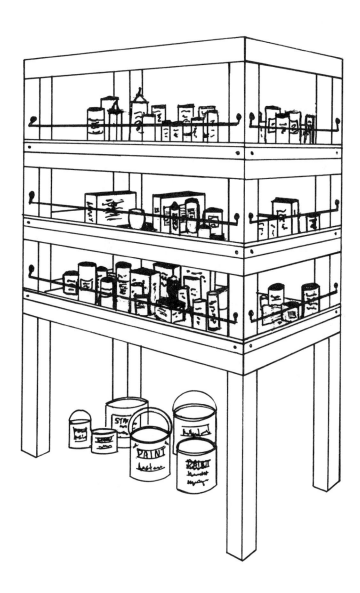

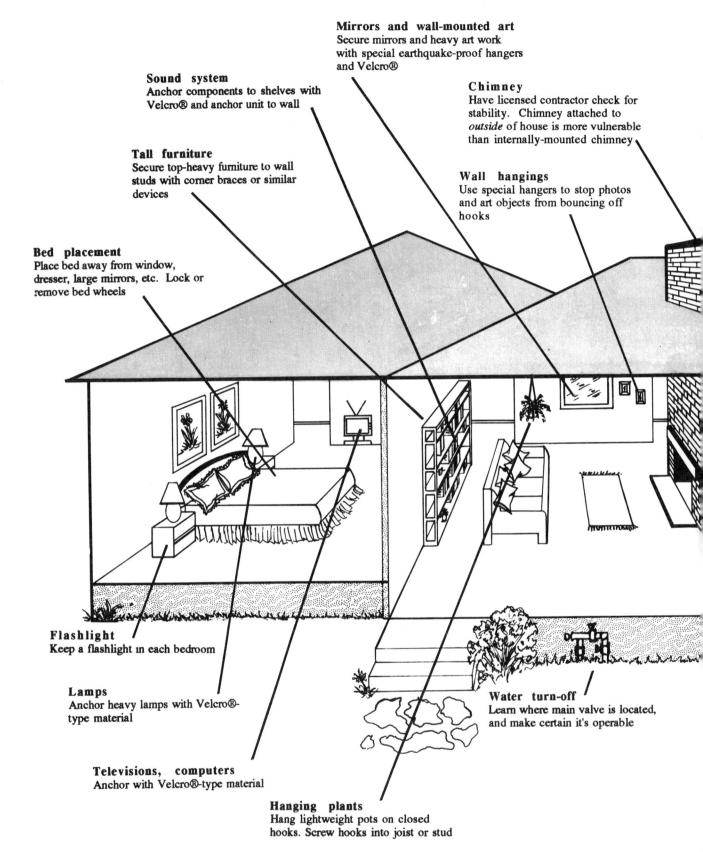

Mirrors and wall-mounted art
Secure mirrors and heavy art work
with special earthquake-proof hangers
and Velcro®

Chimney
Have licensed contractor check for
stability. Chimney attached to
outside of house is more vulnerable
than internally-mounted chimney

Sound system
Anchor components to shelves with
Velcro® and anchor unit to wall

Wall hangings
Use special hangers to stop photos
and art objects from bouncing off
hooks

Tall furniture
Secure top-heavy furniture to wall
studs with corner braces or similar
devices

Bed placement
Place bed away from window,
dresser, large mirrors, etc. Lock or
remove bed wheels

Flashlight
Keep a flashlight in each bedroom

Lamps
Anchor heavy lamps with Velcro®-
type material

Water turn-off
Learn where main valve is located,
and make certain it's operable

Televisions, computers
Anchor with Velcro®-type material

Hanging plants
Hang lightweight pots on closed
hooks. Screw hooks into joist or stud

30

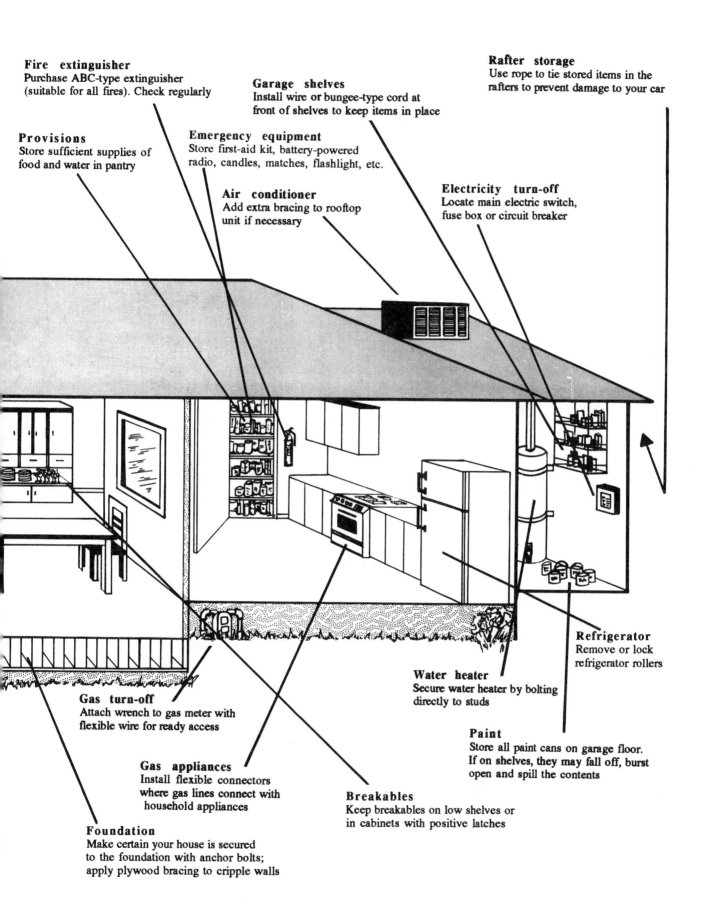

Fire extinguisher
Purchase ABC-type extinguisher
(suitable for all fires). Check regularly

Garage shelves
Install wire or bungee-type cord at
front of shelves to keep items in place

Rafter storage
Use rope to tie stored items in the
rafters to prevent damage to your car

Provisions
Store sufficient supplies of
food and water in pantry

Emergency equipment
Store first-aid kit, battery-powered
radio, candles, matches, flashlight, etc.

Air conditioner
Add extra bracing to rooftop
unit if necessary

Electricity turn-off
Locate main electric switch,
fuse box or circuit breaker

Refrigerator
Remove or lock
refrigerator rollers

Gas turn-off
Attach wrench to gas meter with
flexible wire for ready access

Water heater
Secure water heater by bolting
directly to studs

Paint
Store all paint cans on garage floor.
If on shelves, they may fall off, burst
open and spill the contents

Gas appliances
Install flexible connectors
where gas lines connect with
household appliances

Breakables
Keep breakables on low shelves or
in cabinets with positive latches

Foundation
Make certain your house is secured
to the foundation with anchor bolts;
apply plywood bracing to cripple walls

PREVENTING STRUCTURAL DAMAGE TO YOUR HOME

The California Seismic Safety Commission says that it costs up to 23 times more to repair a quake-damaged house that's not anchored to its foundation and that 1.2 million of the 10 million homes in California are prone to earthquake damage because they're not bolted to their foundations or properly braced.

Since the most costly damage is caused when a house is shaken from its foundation, it's wise to minimize that possibility. When a house is shaken from its foundation, not only is it likely to suffer structural damage, but water and gas pipes might be broken. It's not uncommon for homes to suffer water damage or worse—for ruptured gas lines to ignite. Few realize that most of the massive destruction and loss of property during the 1906 San Francisco earthquake was caused by the resulting fires, rather than the shaking.

It is generally agreed that it was the Long Beach earthquake of 1933 which spurred the state to develop more stringent building codes. While some houses built in the first 3-4 decades of this century might have been securely anchored, it's unlikely.

In 1949, California once again increased the requirements of its building code. So one might reasonably assume that any house built after 1949 would be properly secured, right?

Not necessarily. To make their point, experts point out that although the building code has included specifics regarding the anchoring of homes for something like fifty years, there are numerous homes where the anchorage was not provided or was only partially provided.

Most of us live in single-story wood-frame houses which are the safest type of structures in which to endure an earthquake for two reasons: (a) they're relatively lightweight; (b) their internal walls offer considerable strength as a result of the cross-bracing. But in the case of single-story homes not built directly on a concrete slab, there's usually only a perimeter wall between the first floor and the foundation. This "cripple wall", as it is known, consists of short, vertical studs which connect the concrete foundation to the house's floor joists. In many cases, it may not be adequately braced.

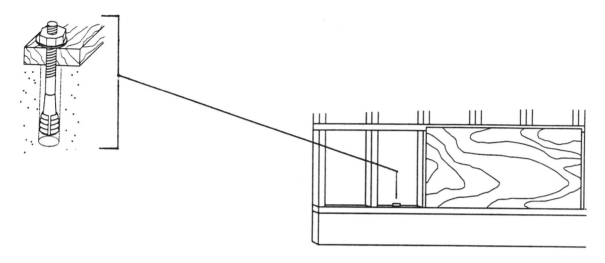

Present code specifies that there should be adequate *shear transfer* to the foundation and suggests methods which are acceptable for this purpose. However, some experts feel that the techniques are, at times, loosely applied. Even more to the point is the fact that we homeowners simply shouldn't rely upon Building Codes to protect us. They vary from region to region and many experts consider them only minimally effective in meeting some earthquake hazards. Keep in mind that Codes are the *minimum* acceptable standards. And if you live in a seismically active region, that may simply not be enough.

Multiple-story homes present a similar problem related to the space beneath the structure's first residential floor. Often, this sub-residential area is used as a garage and garages, by their very nature, lack internal walls which would offer stability to the structure. That means that unless the perimeter walls of such open areas are properly reinforced, they are vulnerable to the possibility of collapse during a major earthquake.

So what should the average homeowner look for? Experts recommend the following:

(1) Crawl beneath your house, if necessary, and check to see if the builder installed 1/2 to 3/4 inch round bolts every six feet around its entire perimeter, thereby attaching the house to the concrete foundation. Such bolts are required by code so if you do not see them, it's strongly recommended that this become your top priority. Because installation of anchor bolts involves using a heavy duty drill to drill holes straight down into the concrete foundation in what is often very cramped quarters, you might want to consider hiring a licensed contractor to do the job for you. Under any circumstances, **be sure to check with the appropriate local authorities to make certain you're satisfying code requirements.**

(2) Check to see if the cripple walls are adequately braced. Although there are a few different ways to brace cripple walls, the one most often recommended involves nailing 3/8 or 1/2 inch structural grade plywood (using 3", 8d 10d nails spaced 4 inches apart) to the inside of all of the cripple wall's studs (verticals) and adjacent joists (horizontals) around the entire perimeter of the house. By doing so, you're creating *shear walls.* It's not even necessary to do this to 100% of the cripple walls. Some experts use a formula based on creating 1 foot of shear wall for every 125 square feet of living area in the house above. (Be sure to add in square feet of the second floor if there is one.) Shear wall board need not be in continuous runs either. It's okay to use pieces as small as 4 feet wide, spaced as needed to bypass plumbing entrances, fireplaces, etc. Last thing: drill 1 1/2 inch ventilation holes for each cavity between studs. Shear wall creation is simple carpentry and can be done by most do-it-yourselfers.

(3) While anchor bolts attach cripple walls to the foundation and shear walls significantly minimize the risk of cripple wall collapse, some experts feel there's still more that can and should be done to stabilize a house. They recommend installing "hold-downs" at the end of each section of shear wall (to attach the bottom of vertical studs to the horizontal sill plate), and "reinforcing angles" to attach the top plate of shear wall studs to upper horizontal rim joists (16 inches on center over the entire length of shear wall). The installation of "hold-downs" and "reinforcing angles" involves drilling into concrete and wood, and often necessitates the installation of additional short-length 2 x 4's to build up areas for attachment and in general.

If crawling around in the dirt beneath your house is not your style, or if you're doubtful you would know what to look for even if it were, you might consider hiring a structural engineer to do it for you. Upon completion of his investigation, he'll hand you a detailed written report. If you wish, he'll also arrange to have the work done for you.

How much will it cost? It's not cheap. Extensive retrofitting can easily run into thousands of dollars. Still, the pound of prevention may prove to be well worth it, as homes may suffer damage in the tens of thousands of dollars following "The Big One".

The table which follows gives information regarding the source of help and possible cost and time needed for some preventative retrofitting projects.

Job	Est. Cost	Hire	Time Required
Get a written evaluation of work needed to secure your house	$350 to $500	Structural engineer	3 to 5 hours
Bolt the house's wood frame to concrete foundation & reinforce cripple walls	$1,750 to $4,000	Licensed contractor	1 week
Add "hold-downs" & "reinforcing angles" to cripple walls	$1,500 to $2,500	Licensed contractor	2 days
Add a concrete foundation & anchor it to house supported by brick or stone piers or a failed foundation	$150 to $300 per foot	Licensed contractor	1 month
Reinforce a house made of brick or stone	$3,000 to $8,000	Masonry contractor	6 to 7 days
Reinforce & anchor a brick fireplace in 1 or 2 story house	$4,000 to $9,000	Masonry contractor	6 to 7 days

Another way to estimate the cost of a comprehensive strengthening project (provided that foundation replacement is not needed and decay/termite damage is not a problem) is to estimate between 2-4% of the home's present value.

Note: Mobile homes are extremely vulnerable to damage during earthquakes. A list of state certified bracing systems specifically for mobile homes is available from the State Department of Housing and Community Development.

How To Locate Qualified Engineers

One source for locating qualified engineers in California is the Structural Engineers Association of California (S.E.A.O.C.), which has prepared lists of engineers who conduct evaluations. Their offices are located as follows:

S.E.A.O.N.C. - Northern California Office
50 First Street, Suite #300
San Francisco, CA 94105
(415) 974-5147

S.E.A.O.C.C. - Central California Office
P.O. Box 2590
Fair Oaks, CA 95628
(916) 965-1536

S.E.A.O.S.D. - San Diego Office
P.O. Box 26500, Suite #203
San Diego, CA 92126
(619) 223-9955

S.E.A.O.S.C. - Southern California Office
5360 South Workman Mill Road
Whittier, CA 90601
(310) 908-6131

S.E.A.O.C. - State of California
1050 Fulton Ave. #150
Sacramento, CA 95825
(916) 427-3647

How To Locate Qualified Contractors

Like doctors, contractors specialize in certain types of work. If you're planning to hire a contractor, make sure he has performed the type of work you want to have done on your home. Don't be reluctant to ask for references from former clients, architects or engineers. Make calls to find out if they were satisfied with the quality of service as well as the price.

Once you've located the contractor you want to do the work, have him write it up in a contract so that both parties have a clear understanding of what will be done, how it will be done, how long it is expected to take and how much it will cost. One more thing: don't agree to any structural work that will not be performed under the supervision of a licensed engineer.

Be leery of anyone who pressures you into signing a contract right away. That's a scam often used by rip-off artists who don't want to allow you time to research their credentials. By contrast, legitimate contractors always allow the customer time to research their qualifications.

There are several ways to locate a competent, qualified contractor:

- (1) Obtain personal references from friends and family members.
- (2) Obtain references from other trades people such as architects and engineers.
- (3) Obtain references from construction suppliers.

To make sure your contractor is licensed and to check whether any complaints have been filed against him or her contact the Contractor's State License Board at (800) 321-2752. You can also determine if the contractor has workers' compensation for employees. Without it, the homeowner may be liable for any injuries to the contractor or his workers incurred while they are on your property.

Note: Check the Appendix for videos which show in detail the process of securing one's house to its foundation.

6

PRACTICE TURNING OFF THE GAS AT THE METER*

People are often surprised to learn that most of the destruction which results from earthquakes is actually caused by fires. And fires are often the result of broken utility lines—more particularly, the gas line. If a house shakes and bounces violently or, worse yet, if it is jostled from its foundation, it's realistic to assume that a gas pipe might break. Obviously, this can produce a potentially volatile situation.

If that should happen, that's no time to be running around looking for a wrench and trying to remember how to turn off the gas supply line to your house because literally *every second* counts. So it's wise to select a wrench *now* and *place it near the gas meter.* It might even be a good idea to use a piece of thin wire to secure it right to the meter itself, just to make certain it stays there.

It's also a good idea to actually practice turning the meter off in advance, because you'll not only want to know how to do it, but your practice session will also serve to free up the valve which may have become frozen with the passing of time.

Here's how to practice turning off the gas main into your home

1. Gather together those persons you believe should know how to shut off the gas supply to your home in the event of a leak. Locate and identify the gas meter and main shut-off valve.

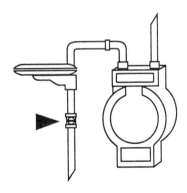

2. Using a 12" adjustable wrench or any other appropriate wrench with a long enough handle to allow you to apply needed pressure, turn the valve *no more than 1/8 turn* either left or right from its vertical position and back again. This may at first be difficult. **CAUTION:** Be careful not to turn the main shut-off valve more than 1/8 turn to the left or the right when practicing. Although a 1/8 turn will not turn the gas off, more of a turn *will*.

3. Check pilot lights and/or gas appliances in the building to see if they are still operating. If you have accidentally shut your main gas valve off and you are familiar with the methods for safely relighting your appliances, slowly turn the main gas valve back on and light the pilots. If you need and call the Gas Company to restore service to your building.

4. If you find that the main shut-off valve is *too difficult* to turn or you are unable to turn it at all, call the Gas Company and request that they come out to adjust or replace it for you.

This advance planning and practice session might save your family and your home.

---

* A major expense in every major earthquake involves the time that the gas company must spend turning the gas back on after people have mistakenly shut it off. Gas service to your home should be shut off *only* if one of the three criteria listed in the chapter entitled *When The Shaking Stops* is met.

7

AUTOMATIC GAS SHUT-OFF VALVES

Most safety experts agree that fires caused by earthquakes often do more damage than the earthquakes themselves. While Japan has for some time mandated that its buildings have automatic gas shut-off valves, the State of California has not yet taken such a step. In fact, historically, gas companies have been reluctant to endorse requiring automatic shut-off valves for residences because they said they were concerned about widespread service interruptions following an earthquake. (Gas companies will send someone to turn on the gas after an earthquake, regardless of whether it was shut off by hand or by an automatic valve. Experts predict, however, that in the event of a major earthquake, it might take a couple of weeks for the gas company to visit your home to restore service.)

Still, many private businesses, hospitals, hotels, schools and government buildings throughout the State of California have installed such valves. Even the Los Angeles City Fire Department has had automatic shut-off valves on some of its fire stations for years and all new fire stations are automatically fitted with them. As what might be considered a statement of endorsement, some insurance companies are known to give discounts to a homeowner's insurance policy when an automatic gas shut-off valve has been installed.

Although to date California gas companies have assumed a "no comment" position regarding the valves, that may change soon. There are indications that at least one gas company in southern California is planning to enter the market and begin both selling and installing units perhaps within a year or so. Recently, the city of Los Angeles passed a bill to take effect in July of 1995 which will require that all new homes and businesses within the city be equipped with automatic gas shut-off valves.

Since January 1, 1987, manufacturers of automatic gas shut-off valves have been required to submit their products for testing and approval by the state, which also conducts quarterly inspections to ensure that they continue to meet the requirements. It's most important that consumers not purchase automatic gas shut-off valves unless they display the seal of the office of the state architect.

Manufacturers of gas shut-off valves use systems of various designs to stop the flow of gas into a home during an earthquake measuring approximately 5.3 to 5.5. Because the internal mechanism's design varies considerably from manufacturer to manufacturer, prospective buyers are encouraged to contact three or more manufacturers for printed information containing product specifications before making their final selection.

Automatic gas shut-off valves should be installed by a licensed plumber or, at the very least, by someone with a plumbing background who is familiar with gas. Check with the Building and Safety Department of your community to find out if you are required to have a permit to install an automatic gas shut-off valve. While you have them on the line, ask whether any additional reports must be filed or permits obtained before beginning installation.

Licensed Manufacturers

Gas shut-off valves range in cost from about $150 to $500 depending upon the manufacturer's particular design. Presently, automatic shut-off valves are manufactured by the following companies who have received state approval for their products:

ACSCO Products Inc.
313 North Lake St.
Burbank, CA 91502
(818) 953-2240

Dove Industries
7016 Marcelle St.
Paramount, CA 90723
(310) 630-0990

Earthquake Safety Systems, Inc.
2064 Eastman Ave., Suite 102
Ventura, CA 93003
(805) 650-5952

Engdahl Enterprises
2930 Grace Lane, Suite E
Costa Mesa, CA 92626
(714) 540-0398

EQ Products, Inc.
11097 Via Temprano
San Diego, CA 92124
(619) 279-9619

Flo-Loc Control Systems, Inc.
226 Calle Pintoresco
San Clemente, CA 92672
(714) 498-7310

Pacific Seismic Products, Inc.
Mfgrs. *California* (aka *Koso)* Seismic Shut-off valve
1436 S. Bentley Ave. #6
Los Angeles, CA 90025
(310) 473-2316 or (800) 978-7263

Quake Defense Inc.
839-A Hinckley Rd.
Burlingame, CA 94010
(800) 969-1906

Quakemaster Inc.
1370 S. Acacia Ave.
Fullerton, CA 92631
(714) 956-5311

Safe-T-Quake, Inc.
16270 Raymer Street
Van Nuys, CA 91406
(818) 989-0753

Seismic Safety Products, Inc.
9225 Ulmerton Rd.; Unit G
Largo, FL 34641
(813) 588-9393; (800) 948-3782

Vanguard Earthquake Valve
534 Leweling Blvd., Suite F
San Leandro, CA 94576
(510) 357-5038

8

FOOD AND WATER

Hardware Items Necessary for Food Preparation

You'll need to have the following cooking hardware readily available in the event of an earthquake:

✓ Heat source (barbecue, hibachi, camp stove or Sterno™)

✓ Fuel for cooking (charcoal, lighter fluid)

✓ Pots

✓ Non-electric can opener

✓ Heavy duty aluminum foil

✓ Paper plates

✓ Plastic knives, forks, spoons

✓ Paper towels

✓ Plastic cups

Experts tell us that, following a major earthquake, we may have to be entirely self-sustaining for at least 3 days, meaning that it is imperative that we stock sufficient food and water supplies. The following types of items are recommended:

Food

✓ Canned or pre-cooked food which requires minimum heat and water.
 Recommended: pasta, rice, canned fruit, canned vegetables, canned

meat, canned fish, canned poultry, canned stew, canned or dried beans, soup, dry cereal, canned nuts, granola bars, canned all-purpose biscuits, peanut butter, powdered or canned milk

✓ Remember special diets for infants and the elderly

✓ Food for household pets

Water

✓ Water (2 quarts to 1 gallon per person per day)

NOTE: See chapter entitled *All About Drinking Water* for information regarding other water sources and water sterilization techniques.

9

EMERGENCY SUPPLIES

Here's a check-list of supplies which will be of value in the hours and days following a major earthquake.

Medications *(Be sure to buy only most current dated stock and rotate as needed)*
✓ Antibiotic ointment
✓ Necessary medications (prescriptions, etc.)
✓ Aspirin and/or pain relief medication
✓ Diarrhea medication
✓ Laxatives
✓ Eye drops
✓ Cough medicine
✓ Antihistamine
✓ Insect spray
✓ Ear and nose drops

Dressing Materials
✓ Band-Aids®
✓ Ace bandages
✓ Butterfly bandages
✓ Gauze pads (4" x 4")
✓ Cotton swabs
✓ Adhesive tape (2")
✓ 2" & 4" wide sterile bandage roll
✓ Triangular bandage for sling, etc. (37" x 37" x 52")
✓ Tongue depressors (popsicle sticks work well)

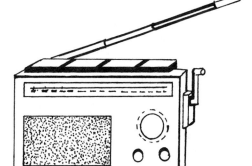

Other Household Items
✓ Baking soda
✓ Bar soap
✓ Book: *Standard First Aid and Professional Training,* by the American Red Cross
✓ Chemical "ice" pack which turns cold when activated
✓ Tweezers
✓ Scissors
✓ Needle and thread
✓ Safety pins

✓ Powder or lotion for sunburn treatment
✓ Sunscreen lotion
✓ Sanitary napkins (may also be used as a compress)
✓ Spoons
✓ Knife
✓ Paper and pencil
✓ Medicine dropper
✓ Thermometer
✓ Facial tissues
✓ Bandage material (strips of sheeting)
✓ Rubbing alcohol
✓ Paper cups
✓ Smelling salts
✓ Space blanket
✓ Matches

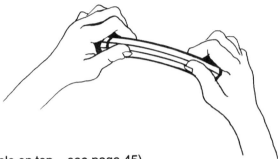

Plus

✓ Portable radio (some available with solar panels on top—see page 45)
✓ Several flashlights
✓ Lightsticks (non-flammable green light source shown at right)
✓ Alkaline batteries (store them in the refrigerator)
✓ Blankets
✓ Food—enough for 72 hours to one week. Include canned goods, powdered milk, dehydrated foods and foods which need no water to prepare. (Include a non-electric can opener.) If you have small children who require special prepared foods, be sure to stock enough food for them too. (Don't forget your pets!)
✓ 3 gallons of water per person in household. (See chapter entitled *All About Drinking Water* for more information)
✓ Pipe and crescent wrenches (to turn off water heater and gas lines)
✓ An alternate cooking source (barbecue, charcoal, starter fluid and matches)
✓ A tarp or tent
✓ Extra pair of eyeglasses if needed
✓ A small bottle of chlorine bleach or water purification tablets (used to disinfect water)
✓ An ABC fire extinguisher (ABC= all fire types)
✓ Plastic bags—the largest available. They can double as wind-breakers, ponchos or even makeshift shelters
✓ Twist-ties
✓ Toilet paper
✓ Shampoo
✓ Toothbrush and toothpaste and dental floss
✓ A watertight container which can be used as an emergency toilet. (Use powdered chlorinated lime or household disinfectant to deodorize and keep insects away)
✓ Thick soled shoes
✓ Heavy work gloves to prevent injury from broken glass and debris

What if your house collapses? The police or fire department may not let you back inside, even to collect your food, clothing or emergency supplies. What if you're at work when a disaster occurs? You might not get help for days. In either case, all you'll have is that kit stashed in your car. See chapter entitled *Automobile Survival Kit Contents* for additional information.

10

FAMILY SAFETY PLANS

It's good to take time to discuss with family members what everyone should do in the event of an earthquake. Here are a few hints that should prove valuable to you and your family.

✔ Locate safe places to be during an earthquake. It's best to get under something sturdy like a desk or table. Next best is to sit against inside walls and cover your head with your arms.

✔ Stay away from windows, mirrors, skylights and furniture that might fall on you.

✔ Teach all family members to **Duck, Cover and Hold!** (See chapter entitled *During an Earthquake.)*

If The Children Are At School

✔ Call your children's school and daycare centers *now* and discuss plans of action to be followed in the event of an earthquake. If an earthquake strikes, it's possible you'll be unable to telephone the school.

Special Instructions for Children

✔ Children should be taught that if they are alone during an earthquake, they should plan to let their family know they are okay. If either the parents or the children are away from home, it might be impossible to locate one another. That's why children should be asked to memorize the phone number of a friend or relative in another town so they can call that party and let them know they are okay. (Often, local lines may be down but long distance lines continue to function.) Then, adult family members will be able to call that number to learn about their children's welfare. Write the person's name, address and phone number on an emergency card that can be included in school, office and car kits, wallets, glove compartments and other handy locations. Also provide the information to your employer and to school teachers and daycare providers. Remember to include coins and calling card numbers for phone calls in such emergencies.

✔ Children should be taught the odor of natural gas so they can identify a leak. And, providing they are old enough (and physically strong enough), children should be taught how to turn off gas and water outside the house.

✔ Children should be instructed to stay away from downed electrical lines outside the house.

✔ Providing they are old enough, children might be shown the master switch inside the electric panel located outside the house.

✔ Children should be told to watch for falling trees and building rubble. Wide open spaces are safest.

✔ Children should be told *not* to return to a damaged house to rescue pets or possessions.

✔ Children should be taught to put on hard soled shoes immediately following an earthquake.

Neighborhood Plans

✔ Get your neighborhood residents together and devise a plan of action.

✔ Gather at least once each year to review and update the plans periodically as well.

The Need for Cash

After an earthquake you'll likely need **cash** for virtually *everything.*

✔ Bank and ATM computers may be out of order so the money you have there may be unavailable for several days.

✔ Grocery stores, unable to process credit card purchases or verify checking account balances because of the loss of electricity, will try to service customers' needs even while the store is closed for clean-up. They do this by moving basic goods (water, batteries, toilet tissue and the like) to the front of the store or to the sidewalk where they operate out of old-time cash boxes. If you need food, the only way you'll be able to buy it will be with *cash.* (Caution: other stores will have the same problem!)

✔ Gas stations without electricity can't pump gas. That's why you should never allow your gas tank to fall below 1/4 full!) In time—perhaps a few days—stations will begin to operate again but once again, they're likely to accept cash and only cash.

Note: 1 Although price-gouging is illegal, it nonetheless occurs following every catastrophic event. That means you might be forced to pay many times the actual value of the product you need. (Gougers are often caught and prosecuted, but most often weeks or months later.)

Note 2: The author recommends that a family of 3 have no less than $300-$500 of cash stashed to see them through the difficult days which follow a major earthquake.

Stash Important Documents

✔ After a major earthquake, you will need vital personal information for a variety of reasons including everything from the processing of insurance claims to disaster assistance applications. Keep the following items and documents and/or information about them in a safe deposit box or another safe place:

- Birth certificates
- Credit cards
- Deeds
- Driver's licenses
- Employment paycheck stubs
- Health histories
- Insurance policies
- Inventory (and photos) of cars, home, household goods, for insurance claims
- Marriage and death certificates
- Mortgage or rental receipts
- Recent income tax returns
- Recent photos of family members for identification in case of separation
- Savings and checking account books
- Small valuables including cameras, watches, jewelry, etc.
- Social security cards
- Stocks and bonds
- Wills

49

NEIGHBORHOOD PLANNING

Imagine having your house survive an 8.3 earthquake with little damage because you secured it properly to the foundation and installed an automatic gas shut-off valve which shut off the gas to your house when the main line ruptured.

Unfortunately, your neighbor's house caught fire which leaped to your home, causing it to burn to the ground.

What a sad scenario. That's why, once you've secured your own home, you should talk to your neighbors about developing a plan which might save the entire neighborhood from devastating losses.

Most cities are eager to help neighborhoods prepare for such disasters, because they realize city services will likely be overwhelmed. Check with your city and county disaster-coordinating agencies, plus the American Red Cross to see what type of cooperation and assistance is available.

A neighborhood meeting scheduled once a year might be all that's needed to protect your properties. In fact, disaster planning might be a natural extension of a Neighborhood Watch Program with which your local police department will assist.

Make sure your neighbors are individually and collectively prepared to assume responsibilities which extend beyond individual property lines. Handicapped and elderly people, as well as infants and pets, require special attention.

Everyone should know where utility shut-offs are located for their immediate neighbors. And if the neighborhood contains people with special skills, like nurses, plumbers, electricians, cellular phone owners, etc., that information should be made available to all.

Some cities have special emergency preparedness teams which can come to scheduled block meetings to explain what planning is in place in your community, help set up a neighborhood plan, and distribute important printed information.

Private emergency-preparedness trainers are available for schools, offices, etc. Check with your city police and fire departments or offices of emergency services for this information.

PREPAREDNESS IN MOBILE HOMES AND APARTMENTS

People who live in community surroundings have a considerable advantage when planning for the eventuality of an earthquake: they can develop a plan in which everyone's responsibilities are clearly defined. This is important because following a major earthquake, fire, police, paramedics and hospital staffs will be stretched to the limit. Telephone service may be disrupted as well. Worse yet, it may be days or even weeks before they will be operating a full capacity again. For that reason, planned cooperation could make mobile homes and apartments much safer places to live in earthquake country.

Those who own or manage apartment complexes and mobile home communities have a responsibility to promote neighborhood preparedness because there is a potential to reduce personal injuries, prevent loss of life *and* significantly reduce property damage.

Preparedness in mobile home communities and apartment complexes begins with an awareness of the community's earthquake-related hazards and risks. This includes arranging a meeting to find out which community members possess skills which will be useful before and after an earthquake, and identifying those who might need special help following a cataclysmal event.

The Plan

Select a community leader
This might be the owner, the manager or simply a resident volunteer. This person's responsibilities will include the following:
1   Contact local police, fire department and Red Cross office and request printed materials for residents.
2   Arrange the resident meeting to acquaint residents with program objectives; distribute printed materials.
3   Arrange for emergency-service officials to visit with residents and assist with making emergency plans.
     organize community 'drills'

4   Motivate the community and help maintain the level of interest.

Select block/floor leaders
No special skills required here, just a sincere interest in making the program work when needed!

1   Learn the special needs and the skills of those in your designated area. Type up the list, complete with names and room of unit numbers, and distribute it to those in your section.
2   Monitor preparedness in the section. For instance, make sure stairwells are clear, exit doors are clearly identified, fire extinguishers are in operating condition, emergency lighting has been installed.
3   Teach preparedness techniques to those in your section.
4   Form search and rescue teams.
5   Help carry out drills.
6   Learn how to turn off gas, water and electricity if needed.
7   Report to the community leader.

Emergency Supply Coordinator
This individual is in charge of stocking and maintaining community emergency supplies.

First Aid Specialists
These people must possess or be willing to seek training in First Aid techniques.

1   Assist in gathering first aid supplies for the community.
2   Make certain First Aid supplies are stored in easy-accessible location.
3   Make sure that First Aid supplies which age are routinely replaced.
4   During a drill, work with block/floor leaders in search and rescue missions.
5   Report to Emergency Supply Coordinator.

Communications Coordinator
This person will be in charge of reaching out beyond your community to the city as needed. He/she must have a ham radio and an emergency power supply.

1   Locate and record all emergency frequencies serving your area.
2   Establish preliminary contact with area emergency agencies and let them know how to reach you as well.
3   Participate in drills.

Family Plan
1   Know how to evacuate without using the building's elevators.
2   Learn how to shut off gas, water and electricity in your family's unit. Teach other family members how to do it also.
3   Design plan for reuniting family members.
4   Make sure everyone, including the children has memorized the telephone number of an out-of-state contact in case family members are scattered when the earthquake strikes.

5   Store sufficient food, water and medical supplies in the house to maintain your family for at least 3 days.
6   Keep a flashlight in *every* room.
7   Keep a battery-powered radio with fresh batteries in storage.
8   Store additional food and medical supplies in the family automobile.

Dangers In The Mobile Home or Apartment

Beware of the following:
- ✔ hanging plants which can swing or come off hooks
- ✔ bookcases and china closes which might topple on you or block your exit
- ✔ mirrors and pictures which can fall and break
- ✔ heavy objects on high shelves
- ✔ kitchen cupboards (install safety latches as described in the *Hardware* chapter)
- ✔ appliances which will move and possibly snap gas, water and electric lines
- ✔ doors which might become immovable (keep a crowbar in the bedroom closet)

Special Water Heater Information

If your mobile home or apartment has an individual water heater, you should make certain it is properly secured. Metal *plumbers tape* wrapped around the water heater and then secured into a strong support inside the wall with a lag bolt will help stabilize your unit. This is important not only to prevent the possible breakage of the gas and water lines but also because by keeping the unit intact you will have secured a safe water supply for your family. (To draw water, first open a hot water tap inside the home.)

If your apartment house gets its water supply from a central water heating unit, make certain it has been secured as well. Your local gas company will supply current literature advising how the job can best be accomplished. Some gas companies will even do the job for a fee!

Things You'll Need In An Emergency

Water
Water mains and service lines often break during an earthquake. Be sure to have stored an adequate supply to maintain your family for at least 72 hours and change it every 6 months.

See the chapters entitled *Food And Water* and *All About Drinking Water* for additional information.

Food
A refrigerator without electrical service will stay cold for up to 24 hours providing you don't open the door. Eat food that will spoil first. Be sure to rotate canned food every 6 months.

See the chapter entitled *Food and Water* for additional information.

First Aid
Knowledge of First Aid is essential after a large earthquake because medical facilities may be overcrowded, damaged or worse yet, destroyed. Ambulance service may be unavailable as well.

Have a first aid kit and guidebook stored in a safe and accessible place. First Aid information may also be found in the front of your telephone book. The Red Cross offers excellent information and classes on the subject. (See the chapter entitled *Emergency Supplied* for additional information.)

Fire Extinguisher
Buy an ABC-type fire extinguisher. (The ABC designation means it will work on most kinds of fires you're likely to experience in the home.) After a major earthquake, the fire department will likely dedicate its resources to major conflagrations and as a result, homeowners will have to take care of themselves.

Inspect your fire extinguisher regularly because they do discharge with the passing of time. Check your Yellow Pages under the 'fire extinguisher' heading for companies which recharge extinguishers.

Thick-soled Shoes
Keep a pair of thick-soled shoes under your bed. Following a major earthquake there's likely to be broken glass strewn throughout your home. Put the shoes on *immediately* after the shaking stops and before you take one step!

Flashlights and "Lightsticks"
Stash a working flashlight in *every* room. Also recommended: lightsticks which are often sold at camping supply stores. They offer a pleasant green light for up to 12 hours without generating any heat or flame. Best of all, they don't deteriorate when stored. Keep at least a dozen stashed throughout your house.

After a Major Earthquake

1. Be ready for more shaking because aftershocks will probably follow in rapid succession.
2. Put on your thick-soled shoes and begin checking for injuries to other household members.
3. Check for gas leaks and if you smell gas, shut your service off at the meter or ask someone else to do it. Don't turn it off unless you detect a leak, however.
4. Check for broken electrical lines and water lines.
5. Open windows to allow for fumes to escape.

6. Turn on your battery-powered radio for information.
7. *Don't* use the telephone unless essential. Lines should remain open for emergency call.
8. *Don't* use elevators

Special Information for Mobile Home Residents

The Northridge earthquake shook more than 10% of the 51,062 residential mobile homes in Los Angeles County from their foundations, rendering them uninhabitable. Another 184 burned to the ground when fires ignited gas which leaked from ruptured lines as homes shifted from their moorings. According to the California Department of Housing and Community Development, more than 1,700 of the severely damaged mobile homes were still considered uninhabitable as much as six months later.

A bill signed in July of 1994, took effect in September that same year which required new mobile homes in California to be tied to the ground in an attempt to help prevent this type of damage. While that's fine for *new* units, the law exempts mobile homes installed before it took effect, the thought being that the exemption would help gain support for the bill from present mobile home owners, many of whom are senior citizens living on fixed incomes.

That exemption, however, will leave the majority of California's mobile homes un-protected unless the owners take the initiative to retro-fit as a safety precaution. The author *strongly* encourages mobile home owners to take that step.

13

Preparedness for The Disabled

Following a major earthquake, fire, police, paramedics, and hospital staffs will be stretched to the limit. It may be days or even weeks before such services will be operating a full capacity again. Even telephone service—that lifeline to the outside world—may be disrupted for hours or days.

Transportation will likely come to a standstill because of the shortage of workers as well as road blockages. Those who rely upon assistance from family members or a nurse may have to do without their help for days following a major earthquake.

For these reasons, it is essential that people with disabilities take precautions above and beyond that required for the general populace.

Planning Ahead

Get to know your neighbors *and* at work, your co-workers. They're likely to be your main source of assistance after an earthquake. More importantly, get to know specific individuals who are willing to help you when a crisis occurs. You'll find ready to offer assistance.

Many people with disabilities hold down jobs away from home. Be sure to advise co-workers of special medical problems and needed medications. Keep available at the work site extra supplies of such medicines or any special equipment you depend on.

Water
Individuals need 2 quarts to 1 gallon of water per person per day. Because water mains and service lines often break during an earthquake, it's essential that you store an adequate supply to maintain you and your family for at least 72 hours. Change the water every 6 months.

See the chapters entitled *Food And Water* and *All About Drinking Water* for additional information.

Food
A refrigerator without electrical service will stay cold for up to 24 hours providing you don't open the door. Eat food that will spoil first. Be sure to rotate canned food every 6 months.

Keep in mind any special dietary restrictions you or members of your family might have.

See the chapter entitled *Food and Water* for additional information.

First Aid
Knowledge of First Aid is essential after a large earthquake because medical facilities may be overcrowded, damaged or worse yet, destroyed. Ambulance service may be unavailable as well.

Have a first aid kit and guidebook stored in a safe and accessible place. First Aid information may also be found in the front of your telephone book. The Red Cross offers excellent information and classes on the subject. (See the chapter entitled *Emergency Supplied* for additional information.)

Fire Extinguisher
Buy an ABC-type fire extinguisher. (The ABC designation means it will work on most kinds of fires you're likely to experience in the home.) After a major earthquake, the fire department will likely dedicate its resources to major conflagrations and as a result, homeowners will have to take care of themselves.

Inspect your fire extinguisher regularly because they do discharge with the passing of time. Check your Yellow Pages under the 'fire extinguisher' heading for companies which recharge extinguishers.

Thick-soled Shoes
Keep a pair of thick-soled shoes under your bed. Following a major earthquake there's likely to be broken glass strewn throughout your home. Put the shoes on *immediately* after the shaking stops and before you take one step!

Flashlights and "Lightsticks"
Stash a working flashlight in *every* room. Also recommended: lightsticks which are often sold at camping supply stores. They offer a pleasant green light for up to 12 hours without generating any heat or flame. Best of all, they don't deteriorate when stored. Keep at least a dozen stashed throughout your house.

Battery Powered Radio
After a major earthquake you'll want minute-by-minute information on the extent of the devastation as well as important warnings might affect you and your neighbors, so keep a battery-powered radio handy. Of course, a car radio will also work but it might not be possible to get to your car.

If you are hard of hearing or deaf, make your disability known to your neighbors so that they will know to relay important information to you.

Medical Supplies
Keep at least a week's supply of medications on hand. Keep items such as bladder pads and catheters in a well-marked container that can be easily transported wherever you go. In an easy-to-locate place, keep a list of essential medications and their prescribed dosages, along with your doctor's name, telephone number and location.

During An Earthquake

Find cover! Stay away from windows, tall furniture and hanging items which might fall and injure you. Move near an interior doorway but don't position yourself where you might get injured if the door swings violently. If possible, get under heavy furniture like a table or bed.

✔ Drop to your knees and protect your head with your arms
✔ Do not try to enter *or* exit a building. Falling debris is one of the most frequent causes of earthquake-related injuries.
✔ If you are out of doors move to a clear area away from poles, signs, buildings or trees.

After a Major Earthquake

✔ Be ready for more shaking because aftershocks will probably follow in rapid succession
✔ Put on your thick-soled shoes and begin checking for injuries to other household members
✔ Check for gas leaks and if you smell gas, shut your service off at the meter or ask someone else to do it. Don't turn it off unless you detect a leak, however.
✔ Check for broken electrical lines and water lines
✔ Open windows to allow for fumes to escape
✔ Turn on your battery-powered radio for information.
✔ *Don't* use the telephone unless essential. Lines should remain open for emergency calls
✔ *Don't* use an elevator

Special Precautions for Those With Impaired Mobility

✔ Plan ahead by letting your neighbors know you may need their assistance in vacating the building. Look for alternate routes
✔ Secure objects (particularly large furniture items) that might fall and block your path
✔ If you are in a wheelchair, stay in it and seek cover in a doorway without a door. Otherwise, position yourself where walls intersect

because there's added structural strength there. Cover your head with your hands.

✔ If you are in bed or out of your wheelchair, seek cover under the bed, a desk or table. If it's not possible to get out of the bed, duck and cover your head beneath the covers

✔ Ask for assistance with exiting. Debris in corridors may block a wheelchair's passage. Your wheelchair may need to be carried downstairs in order to exit the building

Special Precautions for the Deaf or the Hearing Impaired

Because of the nature of this disability, special precautions must be taken. Telephone service will likely be out and as a result, teletypewriters will be useless. If the electricity is also out, your means of communication may be your flashlight. Consider also that people may not realize you cannot hear evacuation warnings and instructions and as a result, may leave you behind. Here's what you will want to do in anticipation of a major earthquake:

Before An Earthquake
✔ Make sure you have a flashlight with good batteries in every room. (Also recommended: lightsticks which are often sold at camping supply stores. They offer a pleasant green light for up to 12 hours without generating any heat or flame. Best of all, they don't deteriorate when stored. Keep at least a dozen stashed throughout your house.)

✔ Keep a pencil and pad next to your bed and another in a room at the other end of the house

✔ Ask a neighbor to be your source of emergency information as it becomes available

During An Earthquake
✔ Watch for falling debris
✔ Drop to your knees and protect your head with your arms

After An Earthquake
✔ Get the attention of others by knocking on doors, banging on walls or striking objects together to make irregular sounds
✔ Put on thick-soled shoes before moving about
✔ Use your flashlight or lightsticks and walk carefully
✔ Have others give you disaster information as it becomes available over radio or battery-powered television

Special Precautions for The Blind
or Those With Impaired Vision

The nature of this disability poses unusual threats both during and after a major earthquake: during the earthquake, you may be injured by falling objects. After the earthquake you may find the usual exits to be obstructed. If you have a seeing-eye dog you may find that the dog is too frightened by the earthquake to be relied upon.

Before An Earthquake
✔ Keep an extra cane at home and another at work even if you have a seeing-eye dog
✔ Memorize alternate escape routes at home and at work. The ones you're accustomed to using may be blocked
✔ Let your neighbors know you'll need their assistance in the event of a major earthquake

During An Earthquake
✔ If you feel the ground shake, assume it's an earthquake and seek cover under heavy furniture or in a doorway which has no door (a swinging door can cause serious injuries) or in a corner
✔ Drop to your knees and protect your head with your arms

After An Earthquake
✔ Put on thick-soled shoes
✔ Use your cane to move about
✔ There will probably be obstructions around you so ask others for help
✔ Get the attention of others by knocking on doors, banging on walls or striking objects together to make irregular sounds. Realize that if electrical service fails after an earthquake, sighted people may not be able to find their way about. Past experience has shown that the sightless can often assist the sighted in such cases
✔ Have others give you disaster information as it becomes available over radio or battery-powered television

14

AUTOMOBILE SURVIVAL KIT CONTENTS

Most of us spend a great deal of time in our vehicles as we travel between our homes, schools and jobs. Following an earthquake, you may be stranded at a location other than your home for as much as 72 hours. Make sure you have enough supplies to meet your needs.

Here's a list of suggested items which should be kept in your car's mobile survival kit:

✔ Nylon carrying bag
✔ Bottled water
✔ Non-perishable food (store in empty coffee cans)
✔ Can opener
✔ Battery-powered radio
✔ Flashlight
✔ Extra *alkaline* batteries
✔ Flares
✔ First Aid Kit
✔ Gloves
✔ Essential medication (if refrigeration isn't required)
✔ Blanket or sleeping bag
✔ Sealable plastic bags
✔ Pre-moistened towelettes
✔ Small package of tissue
✔ Small tool kit (Screwdriver, pliers, wire, knife)
✔ Matches or lighter
✔ Walking shoes and extra socks
✔ Change of clothes (jeans, sweater)
✔ Cash

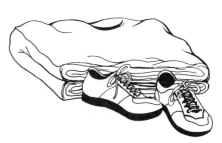

15

EARTHQUAKE INSURANCE

The good news is that earthquake insurance is widely available and, many would say, relatively inexpensive. For instance, the annual per-thousand rate for a single-family wood-frame home in the San Francisco or Los Angeles areas varies from $1.00 to about $4.00, depending upon the location, type of structure, soil conditions, etc. Therefore, the annual premium for $200,000 worth of insurance could be as low as $200 and as high as $800.....not unreasonable when one considers the possible devastation of a major earthquake. (High risk buildings, such as those made of un-reinforced brick, might be rated as high as $11 per $1,000 of coverage.)

The bad news is that nearly all policies have a deductible (usually 10%—but it can be more or less) which is based, not on the *total* of the damage incurred as it is with your automobile policy, but on *the present value of the house itself.*

Here's how a 10% deductible is generally figured:

> Let's say you just paid $200,000 for your house, which, of course, represents the cost of the house plus the land it sits upon. Your earthquake insurance policy shows that the insurance company has declared the house to be worth $160,000 (meaning the land is worth $40,000). In this case, damage to the *structure* would have to exceed $16,000 (10% of $160,000) before the policy would kick in.

> Earthquake insurance policies generally also cover damage or loss to personal property. This is treated separately from damage to the structure. The policy might allow for, say, $90,000 worth of personal property against which a *separate* 10% deductible ($9,000) would apply.

At first glimpse, a loss of that magnitude might seem highly unlikely.... but only until one realizes that most of the damage sustained as a result of the infamous 1906 San Francisco earthquake was said to have been caused by fire, rather than the quake itself.

In fact, fires are to be expected when the earth shakes violently, because gas pipes both inside and outside the home are often broken. And which internal pipe is most vulnerable? The one which leads to your water heater. Water heaters are inherently unstable because of their tall, thin design. That's why you are urged to secure your water heater immediately.

There are other clauses of which you should be aware which sometimes appear in earthquake policies. For instance—

Many policies carry a 72-hour occurrence limit, meaning that you are liable for the deductible *again* on damage which results from a late aftershock.

Some policies exclude quake-related fires, including fires which originate from outside your property—such as a neighbor's burning house.

Until recently, many wondered whether insurance companies would be able to stand behind their policies in the event of a major earthquake. The January 17, 1994 Northridge earthquake answered that question—several companies sustained such devastating losses they either decided it was unwise or found it impossible to continue to serve California's homeowners' insurance market. Insured losses approximated $12 billion with uninsured losses adding at least $8 billion more.

According to the National Committee on Property Insurance that $20 billion might sometime in the not-too-distant future, look like a bargain. Based on what was learned from the Northridge earthquake, they now consider it a real possibility for an earthquake which would strike in or near a major California metropolitan area to cost as much as *$50 billion.*

A lot of questions and a lot of concerns. Still, the author considers earthquake insurance to be a worthwhile expenditure. After all, it's your *second* best line of defense....right after having prepared your house and your family.

If you want earthquake insurance, start by contacting the company which presently insures your dwelling. But don't stop there; shop around.

If you have questions about insurance, call the Department of Insurance at (800) 927-HELP; if you live in the 213, 310 or 818 area codes, call (213) 897-8921. The mailing address is:

The Department of Insurance
300 South Spring Street
Los Angeles, CA 90013

For Those Who Own Rental Properties

Here's a caveat for those who are attempting to build equity through the ownership of rental properties such as apartments, condos, townhouses and even single-family dwellings.

In a major earthquake, rental properties may be damaged so severely that tenants will be forced to vacate the premises. Of course, empty rental properties don't generate income despite the fact that the property's owners will be expected to meet their monthly mortgage payments on time.

Fortunately, there *is* a way rental property owners can protect themselves via an insurance policy *endorsement* which, for an additional premium, will cover "loss of rental income" resulting from an earthquake. It's definitely worth checking into!

For Those Living in
Condos And Townhouses

As a result of the Northridge earthquake, residents of numerous condo and townhouse complexes became painfully aware of some earthquake insurance realities which they had not anticipated.

Some condo structures suffered such extensive damage that their homeowners' associations were forced to initiate "special assessments". (A special assessment is a charge which each condo owner is expected to pay when the condo association's financial reserves are not sufficient to offset unanticipated losses. It amounts to the amount of the deductible on the association's insurance policy, divided among the number of units in the complex.) Such special assessments were occasionally as low as a couple hundred dollars but those who lived in complexes which suffered extensive damage, were billed as much as $10,000 or more!

Residents who were unable to pay that amount from their savings, were forced to seek low-cost loans which carried monthly premiums spread over a period of years. And of course, these payments were in addition to their regular monthly mortgage and association payments.

Had the individual unit owners carried their own earthquake insurance policies in addition to the complex's earthquake coverage, they would have been covered for such things as special assessments, temporary housing, contents damage and much more.

Could it be worse? Unfortunately, the answer is yes. There were numerous cases where within a complex, some condo units were so badly damaged that their owners "walked away", abandoning their condos and their loans. The abandoned loans were the banks' problems, but the abandoned condos became instantaneous headaches for those who remained because the abandoned assessments were then spread among those who remained—on top of their own mortgage, association fee and special assessment fee.

Note: Generally, structural repairs to a condominium building, whether inside or outside an individual unit, are covered under the complex's master policy It is important for unit owners to understand that individual unit owners are technically not "named insureds" under the master policy. That means that the insurance carrier for the master policy will deal with the appointed representatives of the association and payment will be issued to the association. It is then up to the board of directors to distribute funds among the owners. Depending on the extent of the damage and the experts (engineers, contractors, etc.) involved, the claim process can be lengthy.

Unequal Damage

Another issue of concern to condo/townhouse owners is the fact that it's not likely that all buildings in a given complex will sustain damage in equal measure. That means that your building may come through with little or no damage while another is all but trashed. Nonetheless, home-owner association contracts generally stipulate that damages to the complex are to be shared *equally*. While this is fair, it's not always easy to swallow.

16

DURING AN EARTHQUAKE

Above all, try to remain calm. You'll be more capable of assessing the situation and reacting properly.

DUCK
DUCK or drop down to the floor.

COVER
Take COVER under a desk, table or other sturdy furniture. (Doorways are not recommended because a violently swinging door might cause injuries.) If that's not possible, seek COVER against an interior wall and protect your head with your arms. Avoid danger spots near hanging objects, windows, mirrors or tall furniture like bookcases and china cabinets.

HOLD
If you have taken cover beneath a sturdy piece of furniture, HOLD onto it. Stay in that position until the ground stops shaking.

If You Are Indoors...

1. Don't try to leave the building, as you may be subjecting yourself to even greater danger from debris which sometimes falls from building exteriors.
2. Take cover under a desk, table or against an inside wall.
3. Stay clear of glass and other falling debris.
4. Stay away from windows, mirrors, bookcases, file cabinets and fireplaces.
5. Turn off stove burners at first sign of shaking and move away from the refrigerator, stove and cupboards—if possible, move to another room *fast.*
6. If you are in a crowded building, don't rush for the exit, as others will have the same idea. Instead, seek shelter under a table or other stable piece of furniture.

If You Are Outdoors...
*   Get into an open area away from buildings, trees, signs and power lines.

If You Are On A Sidewalk Near Buildings...
*   Duck into a doorway to protect yourself from falling bricks, window glass and other debris.

If You Are In A High-Rise Building...
1. Stay away from windows and outside walls.
2. Remain on the same floor.
3. Do *not* use elevators.
4. Fire alarms, burglar alarms and automatic sprinklers may go on, helping to contribute to the already tense atmosphere. Don't panic.

If You Are In A Crowded Public Place...
1. Move away from display shelves and cases.
2. Do *not* rush to the exit doors.

If You Are In A Stadium Or Theater...
1. Stay in your seat and cover your head with your arms.
2. Do not try to leave until the shaking has stopped and then do so in a calm and orderly manner.

If You Are In An Automobile...
1. Pull over to the side of the road and stop away from power lines, overpasses and bridges.
2. Stay in your car and listen to the radio to assess the situation.

If You Are In A Wheel Chair...
*   Stay in it and move to cover if possible. Lock the wheels and cover your head with your arms.

17

WHEN THE SHAKING STOPS

✓   Expect aftershocks. They commonly follow earthquakes and some may even be as strong as, or stronger than the original quake.

✓   Check for injuries and administer needed care. If a person is seriously injured, do not move him unless he is in immediate danger. Cover him with blankets to prevent loss of body heat.

✓   While wearing heavy-soled shoes, check for fire hazards as well as spilled chemicals, medicines, flammable liquids, etc.

✓   When search is completed, open windows to vent potentially dangerous fumes.

✓   If damage to electrical system is suspected (frayed wires, sparks or the smell of hot insulation), turn off the system at the main circuit breaker or the fuse box.

✓   If water leaks are suspected, turn off water at main valve.

✓   Tune battery-operated radio to news station to learn the extent of damage in your area and to receive emergency instructions and warnings.

✓   Stay away from downed power lines or any objects which are touched by downed wires.

✓   Tape broken windows to prevent glass shards from falling during aftershocks.

Your Utilities

Turn Off The <u>MAIN</u> Gas Shut-off Valve *if*.............

•   —you smell gas *or suspect a gas leak, regardless of whether the building is damaged or undamaged.* Keep in mind that, in the case of houses built on cement slabs, gas pipes are placed in the ceilings. Since gas fumes rise, it's possible in slab-foundation houses there could be a gas leak which would not be detectable by household occupants. (Don't light matches or burners or turn on ANY electrical switches if you have even the *slightest* concern!)

•   —your gas water heater or any other gas appliance has been knocked over and/or pulled free from its connection.

•   —your building has suffered extensive damage, such as large cracks in the exterior walls or in the concrete slab floors, etc. and you suspect the gas lines or appliances have been damaged.

Once you have turned off your gas service, **DO NOT TURN IT BACK ON**! Call the gas company to do it for you. Remember that the gas company may be disrupted for several days and your service will be restored as soon as conditions permit. As an alternative, you may also contact a qualified licensed plumber to have your piping checked and gas service restored.

Turn the valve a quarter turn in either direction so that it runs crosswise to the pipe. The valve is now closed. Turn the valve a quarter turn in either direction so that it runs

WARNING: It is very dangerous and therefore not recommended that you search for gas leaks inside a damaged building.

NOTE: Automatic gas shut-off valves are designed to shut off all gas service to your home in the event of a strong earthquake. See chapter entitled *Automatic Gas Shut-off Valves* for more information.

Turn off the <u>MAIN</u> Water Shut-off Valve *if...*

•   —you locate a leak.

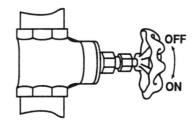

Turn Off The ELECTRICITY At The Breaker Box *if*...

- —you hear sparking sounds or see or smell smoke

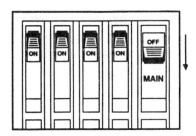

Streets And Highways

- Keep roads clear to allow emergency vehicles access to your area.
- Don't go sightseeing after the quake, as unnecessary traffic can impede emergency vehicles.
- Stay away from beaches and waterfront areas where a tidal wave might strike.

Reuniting Your Family

Have a plan for reuniting the family which does not involve the telephone. Families with children should be aware of their school's evacuation procedures and plan accordingly. Travel may be difficult after a major earthquake.

Disaster Psychology

Following an earthquake, you will likely be very busy cleaning up or perhaps even looking for a new place to stay.

There are some normal reactions we all experience after such an occurrence. Generally these feelings don't last very long, but it is common to feel let down and resentful. Other feelings, listed here, may not appear until weeks or even months after the earthquake:

Anger
Disorientation
Fatigue
Headaches
Hyperactivity
Inability to sleep

Increase in alcohol consumption
Increase in drug consumption
Irritability
Lack of concentration
Loss of appetite
Memory problems
Nausea
Nightmares
Sadness
Startle response to loud noises

Things Which Help To Relieve The Stress of An Earthquake

- Talking about your disaster experiences.

- Taking time off from cares, worries and even home repairs. Save time for recreation, relaxation or your favorite hobby.

- Get away from home with friends for a day or even a few hours.

- Pay attention to your health, to your diet, and make sure you get adequate sleep.

- Prepare for possible future aftershocks to lessen feelings of helplessness.

- Rebuild personal relationships. Couples should make time to be alone together both for talk and fun.

- If stress, anxiety, depression or physical problems continue, you may wish to contact the post-disaster services provided by the local mental health center.

Helping Children Cope With The Disaster

Children are often particularly upset following an earthquake. These feelings are normal and generally do not last long. Here are some of the problems you may see in your children:

✓ Excessive fear of darkness, separation or being alone
✓ Clinging to parents
✓ Fear of strangers
✓ Worry
✓ An increase in immature behavior
✓ Not wanting to go to school
✓ Changes in eating/sleeping habits
✓ Increase in aggressive behavior
✓ Shyness
✓ Bedwetting and/or thumb sucking
✓ Persistent nightmares
✓ Headaches, stomach aches or other physical complaints

Note: A child may revert to "childish" behavior which he/she had outgrown such as wetting the bed, clinging to parents and thumb sucking. This should not alarm parents because they are normally of short duration. They are signs of the child's anxiety and parents' acceptance will reassure the child and shorten the duration of the behaviors. Should parents over-react by becoming overly concerned, punishing or nagging the child, the symptoms may persist much longer. Children respond to praise; parents should make an attempt not to focus on the child's regressive behavior.

Things You Can Do To Help Your Child

✓   Talk with your child about his/her feelings and share your feelings as well.
✓   Talk about what happened at a level the child can understand.
✓   Reassure your child that you are safe and that you will stay together.
✓   Hold and touch him/her often.
✓   Spend extra time alone with your child at bedtime.
✓   Allow your child to grieve over a lost toy, lost blanket or lost home.
✓   If you feel your child is having problems at school, talk to his/her teacher so you can work together to help your child.
✓   If symptoms continue, you may wish to take your child to a children's post-disaster service clinic provided by the local mental health center.

ALL ABOUT DRINKING WATER

The city water supply is vulnerable to the effects of a large earthquake, as contaminants can get into the drinking water supply through ruptures in pipes, through the mixing up of sediments, through the adulteration of filtering systems, etc. If you suspect a problem, use alternate sources of water. Listen for news broadcasts which will likely address administrative concerns about the safety of drinking water in your area.

Sources of Drinking Water

1. **Tap water** can be stored in anticipation of an earthquake. Storage is both practical and economical if you observe the following precautions. Rinse used bleach containers well, then fill them with water. If the water is clear, add 8 drops (1/4 teaspoon) of chlorine (household) bleach* per gallon. (Add 16 drops if cloudy.**) Be sure to seal containers tightly. Water stored like this will last 6 months to a year and then should be replaced. A slight chlorine odor should remain.

2. **Bottled water** may be purchased at the market or delivered directly to your home. Both spring water and distilled water are acceptable; let your taste preference be your guide. The best storage container is the 5-gallon bottle generally used for home delivery. Such containers, when made from polycarbonate, are sturdy and can be stored under almost any conditions. The container should be kept in an upright position out of the sun. Since it will not absorb odors, it can be safely stored in the family garage.

    The 1-gallon size container sold in supermarkets is a good alternative, but the length of storage time is limited due to the need for "ideal" storage conditions. Ideally, the storage area should be cool, dry, of constant temperature and should not be exposed to odors or odor-causing products such as moth balls, soap, gasoline, onions, etc. An ideal location within the home would be a linen closet. Since most homes lack ideal storage conditions, authorities recommend rotating the water at I least every 6 months. Simply use the water on hand and replace it with a new bottle. If you are concerned that the water might take on a plastic taste, you may instead want to rotate the water every three months. (A plastic taste does not necessarily indicate that the water has become unsafe.)

Sealed water packets called "sachets" contain approximately 4.225 oz. of water and have a shelf-life of 5 years. The packets are available at special stores and by mail in cases which contain as many as 60 packets for approximately $12. Check the *Appendix* for sources.

3. **The hot water heater** storage tank contains between 25 and 50 gallons of usable water. To get the water out of the tank it is necessary to turn off the cold water supply to the tank (to prevent contaminated water from the city's system being drawn into the tank as you drain it). Next, open any hot water tap in the house to allow air to enter so the water will flow out. Drain needed water from the bottom of the tank at the drain valve. It's very important to turn off the heat source to the hot water heater before draining water because of the danger of super heating.

4. **The water in the home's piping system** can sometimes be removed using the following procedure. First, locate and shut off the main service valve. Next, locate and open the highest water tap to allow air into the system. The water can be recovered by next locating and opening a lower system water tap and draining the water into a suitable container.

5. **The toilet water storage/flush tank** is another source. To be potable, the water must come from the tank and **not** the bowl. It must not have additives in it. Do *not* drink water colored with chemical agents.

6. **Melted ice cubes** are another source.

7. **Water-packed canned goods** will also suffice.

NOTE: Swimming pool water is *not* acceptable for drinking or cooking purposes. Pool water contains chemicals which, if ingested in any quantity, might put one's health at risk. Swimming pool water *is* acceptable, however, for hygienic uses such as washing clothing and flushing toilets.

Purifying Water Using Heat

1. First, strain dirty water through a coffee filter, cheese cloth or a paper towel to catch any sediments, glass or debris.

2. Boil the water vigorously (five minutes at sea level—up to ten minutes at high altitudes).

3. After cooling, the water is ready to use.

Purifying Water Using Bleach

1.   First, strain dirty water through a coffee filter, cheese cloth or a paper towel to catch any sediments, glass or debris.

2.   Next, follow instructions listed above under **Tap Water.**

Purifying Water Using Iodine

1.   First, strain dirty water through a coffee filter, cheese cloth or a paper towel to catch any sediments, glass or debris.

2.   Add household tincture of iodine (10 drops per gallon), mix well, let stand for 30 minutes.

*Solutions containing active ingredients other than sodium hydrochloride should *not* be used.

**If the water is cloudy, double the dose-per-quantity indicated above.

HUMAN WASTE SANITATION AND DISPOSAL

Following an earthquake, you may discover that as a result of a break in the main supply line, you have no running water. Or, you may be advised via news broadcasts not to flush toilets because sewer lines have been broken. If that happens, you will have to resort to alternative means for handling human waste at your home.

One alternative is to place a plastic bag within the toilet bowl to collect waste. (*Warning: Do not attempt to flush the toilet for the bag could clog the disposal line!*) Following use, a small amount of disinfectant should be added to the bag before sealing it with a twist-tie and placing it in a tightly covered container away from people.

If the toilet itself is unusable for any reason, a plastic bag placed within a bucket may be substituted.

Four types of disinfectants are readily available and easy to use in such circumstances. It is advised that you select one to store with your emergency supplies:

1.   Providing water is available (save drinking water—use non-potable water for waste disposal), a solution of 1 part liquid chlorine bleach to 10 parts water is very effective. Do not substitute dry bleach, which is caustic and not safe for this type of use.

2.   HTH, also known as calcium hypochlorite, is available at swimming pool supply stores. HTH is also intended to be used in solution form. Follow the directions on the package.

3.   Powdered, chlorinated lime, available at building supply stores, can be used dry. Be sure to get *chlorinated* lime and not *quick* lime, which is highly alkaline and corrosive.

4.   Portable toilet chemicals, both liquid and dry, are available at recreational vehicle supply stores and some camping stores. Follow directions on the package.

Warning! Chlorinated products which are intended to be mixed with water can be hazardous if used dry.

LIVING THROUGH THE NORTHRIDGE EARTHQUAKE

Below, residents tell their personal stories.

Like nearly everyone else in the greater Los Angeles area, I was asleep when the earthquake struck at 4:31 a.m. on Monday, January 17, 1994. It would be more than a week before I would learn that my house was just 1 1/2 miles from the epicenter.

There was no gradual build-up. The noise and the shaking were both violent instantaneously. The roar was as loud as if a freight train were passing within feet of the house at full speed, but the movement was far greater. The shaking was so violent I realized it would be hopeless to try to leave the bed so I pulled the quilt up over my head and rode it out.

I was never aware of how dark it can be in this city because city lights always sneak into our homes even with the curtains drawn. Not this time. The darkness was absolute. When the shaking stopped, I decided to remain in bed; I was certain there would be substantial damage throughout the house and I didn't consider it safe to try to find my way in the dark.

The aftershocks, coming frequently as they do, seemed every bit as violent as the earthquake itself , though they didn't last as long. After about an hour I couldn't contain my curiosity any longer, so I decided to get up and take a look at the house. Unfortunately, my flashlights were in the laundry room at the other end of the house, so I would have to find my way there in the darkness. I put on hard soled slippers and groped my way through the house by touching the walls.

As I passed through the living room, I felt cold air and realized a window must be broken. When I reached the kitchen, I saw the faint glow of soft green light coming from something on the floor. As I bent down to pick it up, I could tell it was the receiver from the wall telephone and the light I saw was coming from its keypad. I picked up the receiver and used its faint light at the end of the 9 foot cord to help me find the flashlight in the adjacent laundry room.

I switched on the flashlight and surveyed the damage. Putting it mildly, the kitchen was a mess. The refrigerator was standing 2 feet from the wall, its door open and its contents strewn across the floor. Kitchen cabinet doors had been bounced open and all of the glassware and dinner plates were broken on the floor, mixing with spaghetti sauce, sugar, flour, catsup, oil and other liquids to form a sickening mess.

As I passed through the den, I could see that one of the four sliding glass doors which faced the pool was gone—that's where at least some of the cold air was coming from. The den carpet was soggy from pool water that had sloshed into the house through the hole vacated by the sliding glass door, which I assumed had shattered on the pool deck.
In both the living room and den, formerly recessed fluorescent lights were dangling by their metal flexes, hanging nearly to knee level.

Everything in the living room was on the floor— statues, pictures, artwork and more. A clay pot and a fragile bust of Beethoven, both of which had been on the fireplace mantel were lying 6 feet away, unbroken. The stereo speakers were face down and the CD racks had toppled, unloading a cargo of more than 400 CDs in a heap. Floor and table lamps were lying on the floor, most of them broken. Three recessed lighting fixtures now hung nearly to the floor.

The chandelier above the dining room table had been ripped from the ceiling box and had smashed on the dining table below.

Every item in my home office was on the floor, including the fax machine, television, hundreds of books and papers, scales, lamps—everything. I felt cold air coming in through a 4 x 4 broken window there as well.

On my way back to my bedroom, I glanced into the two guest bedrooms. No surprise there. Everything was on the floor.

Both bathrooms were at least temporarily unusable. One of the toilets had cracked and was leaking. Both had sloshed all the water in the bowls onto the floors, which were also strewn with the broken contents of the medicine cabinets.

With the help of the flashlight, I could finally see my bedroom. What a mess! The cabinet which held the color television and VCR had toppled and smashed both units to pieces. A floor lamp which had stood in the corner was leaning over the bed less than a foot from where my head had lain.

I heard a knock at my front door, then the voices of my neighbors asking if I was OK. I tried to open the door but it was jammed shut. I told them I was fine, so they moved on to check on others.

About 20 minutes later, a nasty aftershock jarred the house and mysteriously un-jammed the front door. I stepped outside in my pajamas and joined neighbors on my front lawn.   We could see others with flashlights leaving their houses for the safety of the street. But it was too cold to stay outside so I returned to the relative comfort of my bed and turned on my battery-powered radio and television to see how bad it was.

It was too early for newscasters to have gathered details but bits and pieces were beginning to be reported and it sounded terrible for the entire city and the surrounding area. Fires could be seen and explosions heard throughout the area Helicopters were beginning to give us real-time pictures of the devastation.

Once the sun was up and it was warmer outside, I noticed that the sliding glass door wasn't broken after all. Amazingly, it had simply been knocked off its track and was leaning at a sharp angle against the outside of the house. With the help of a friend, I got it back onto its track.

I decided my next job was to find someone to replace the broken glass window in my office; otherwise, I would have to suffer through cold winter nights. And without electricity, there would be no furnace to warm the house.

Although my telephone had electricity to light the keypad, there was no dial tone and there wouldn't be for another 2 days. At 9:30, I took the Yellow Pages, a Thomas Brothers map and my cell phone to my car and launched a search for a glass shop that might be open.

I tried calling several on my cell phone. Only a few answered and most of those were owners who had just reached their shops to be faced by heaps of broken glass. Some said they had nothing left; others said they wouldn't know if they had anything usable until afternoon. Still others said that even if they did have glass, they had a contractual obligations to service their commercial customers first. It didn't look good.

Finally, I located one glass shop owner who said he thought he could replace my window that afternoon. Somewhat comforted, I returned home to begin the clean-up.

We had no electricity for 3 days—which meant no heat and no light, which also meant going to bed when it got dark at about 6 p.m. and staying there until the sun came up the following morning. There was also no hot water: even though it was strapped, the water heater had walked some distance across the floor, in the process producing a small leak, so I turned it off and closed the valve. I would find out that thousands of water heaters had tumbled and all of the flex lines in Southern California stores were gone from store shelves that same morning. I finally had some flown in from Arizona 3 days later.

Jeremy Little
University Professor

The noise was almost as bad as the violence of the shaking—like thunder roaring under the house. In my bedroom, glass shattered everywhere, hard objects slammed against the walls. Books, bookcases, television, typewriter hurled across the room into the darkness.

I was thrown out of bed by the impact. When I reached for my flashlight on the night table, it wasn't there—the table, that is. It had flown twelve feet and landed on top of the television which was face down on the floor. When the shaking stopped, I crept through the debris on my hands and knees toward the bedroom door, but the door was blocked by my metal filing cabinet which had pitched over in front of it.

Incredibly, I found my flashlight and with its help managed to scramble over the top of the cabinet and through the narrow opening between it and the door.

Two of the three students who live with me were standing frozen in their doorways. The last one, David, was trapped inside his bedroom downstairs by *his* filing cabinet. When the three of us made it outside, we ripped the screen from his window and pulled him out.

The shaking continued on and off. Together, David and I turned off the main gas line with a wrench I'd left permanently on the meter. David managed to reach back inside his room and get some blankets. We all huddled together on the lawn in the darkness. We were amazed to be alive.

Twenty minutes after the earthquake, the house two doors away exploded; nobody had been home to shut off the gas. The whole area became what I imagine a war zone to be like: helicopters buzzing overhead, sirens screaming all around us. We could hear neighbors yelling for help. One-third of the water in my swimming pool had shot up and out of the pool, drenching the yard. As the ground continued to shake, we watched the house rock violently back and forth.

When light dawned, we mustered the courage to go inside. The air was cloudy with white dust from the ceilings. There was no electricity, no water, no telephone, no gas. The refrigerator had fallen almost on its face, held from the floor at a steep angle only by the confines of the nook into which it was built. Its contents were splattered across the floor, as were the contents of every cupboard and drawer in the kitchen. All 40 of them. We were knee deep in flour, ketchup, soy sauce, jam and broken dishes.

Almost every picture fell from the walls. Every book in the house, hundreds of them along with their bookcases, flew to the floor. Most of my pre-Colombian pottery collection was destroyed as were dozens of antiques. I've since thrown then all away; they're no longer important.

The worst problem was my hydronic boiler furnace with copper coils under all the floors. It's a total loss because the coils were smashed and water began seeping up through the tiles. It's unrepairable as is my copier and one of my computers.

I slept in a tent (or in my car when it rained) for weeks, but at least I survived. I thank God for my three wonderful children as well as my neighbors and friends who helped in every way possible.

Betty Moss
Retired College Teacher

The bed was jumping up and down with jackhammer force. All I could do was grab the mattress with both hands and hang on for dear life.

There must have been a tremendous amount of noise. Furniture was toppling, glassware crashing, books thudding to the floor. But all I remember of the event itself is holding on while the bed bucked like a Brahma bull.

Even so, I remained calm—or thought I did. Once the shaking stopped, I picked my way over heaps of books and continued on, barefooted, across the welter of broken glass that littered the bathroom floor. (I was fortunate to have that second route out of my bedroom; although I didn't know it then, the main door was blocked by fallen furniture.) I emerged—fortunate again—with only a small cut on the bottom of one foot.

Having read *Earthquake Prepared* in its previous edition, I had made *some* preparations for a quake. I was rather proud of myself for having purchased canned food, plastic jugs of water, and two flashlights—all of which were in the pantry, on the other side of the uncrossable sea of broken glass that I knew must cover the kitchen floor.

How I needed a flashlight! I had never realized how dark it could be, with no street or porch lights on for miles around.

I became aware that my two dogs had joined me in the hall. I ran my hands over their fur and was vastly relieved to find that neither had been injured. Then I opened the front door. It was a little lighter outside than in, so I went outdoors. Before long, I came back inside, for no particular reason, then went out again. I still *thought* I was calm, but I kept going in and out, as mindlessly and repetitively as a cuckoo popping in and out of a clock.

On my fourth trip out, my next door neighbors joined me in my front yard. They had a wrench (mine was in the pantry with the flashlights), and went with me to turn off the gas. And bless them!— they had an extra flashlight.

Armed with that, I went back into the house. I decided to let my dogs out into the back yard, as I usually did in the morning. I should have first surveyed the yard; the block wall across the back had tumbled down. At some point, one of the dogs went off exploring. Fortunately, a neighbor brought her back hours later.

Unaware, as yet, of her absence, I made my way into my bedroom. The flashlight let me see, for the first time, what had been happening around me while I clutched the bucking mattress. A large heavy armoire lay tilted against my work table; my laser printer had crashed through a floor-to-ceiling window and rested half inside, half out; the television had flown a good five feet and landed face down on a foot-deep layer of books.

But the worst shock was when I shone the flashlight on the wall above my bed. A large room air conditioner directly over my pillow had walked into the room a good eight inches. Had the shaking lasted any longer, it almost certainly would have fallen on my head.

After seeing that, I stayed only long enough to find my purse, a pair of shoes and a sweat suit. Then I fled the room. It was three weeks before I slept in my bed again. Until I had gotten a handyman to bolt the heavy furniture into the wall and, especially, to secure the air conditioner, not only did I not sleep in there, I could hardly bear to enter the room.

By then, the sun had risen. I managed to get through by phone to reassure my elderly parents, then started at one end of the kitchen, excavating layers of broken glass. When I was done, a few hours later, I saw that a once-complete set of fine china and crystal glassware had been reduced to a single plate and a sherbet goblet.

Clearing the kitchen was the only task I accomplished so quickly. Reaction set in during the ensuing days, and I found it very difficult to force myself to continue the clean-up. Finally, I put myself on a schedule. 30 minutes of clean-up, then a break. Another 30 minutes, another break. Working that way, I got the worst of the wreckage cleared within a week.

Other damage came to light only considerably later: A quadruple-the-usual water bill revealed a leak in the main line leading to the house; weeks after that, I found that yellow jackets had set up housekeeping inside one wall, having entered through a small, quake-caused crack in the exterior stucco.

Still, I was one of the lucky ones. My house came through structurally sound. Most important, neither I nor any of those closest to me had been hurt.

Bit by bit, in the days following the quake, things got better. First, the electricity came back on, then the water, then the gas. The night, three weeks after the quake, when I slept in my bedroom again, I felt as if life was back to normal. Almost.

Only almost—for there are continuing inconveniences and reminders. For me, these include: stores that shut down, some never to reopen; no shopping mall closer than a 30 minute drive; a nearby row of apartment buildings, still fenced-off and boarded-up. Recently, several vacant lots have appeared on my street—the houses on them have been torn down, too badly damaged to be fixed.

Add these vivid reminders to the occasional aftershock, plus the news articles and TV stories, and it makes the quake impossible to forget.

Nor should it be forgotten. I am better prepared now than I was before. With luck, the next time a quake hits, more of the contents of my house will stand. I now keep a pair of shoes beneath my bed, a flashlight under my pillow—and five other flashlights stashed in various locations. Recently, I purchased two earthquake lights, ones that plug into the wall and light up when the power goes off. At least, I figure, when the next one hits—as is almost inevitable here in the earthquake zone—I won't be in the dark for long.

Karen Ervin-Pershing
Teacher, Author

I thought the earth was opening and Los Angeles was falling in. We awoke to a deafening roar and a motion that kept us airborne. I screamed louder and longer than I ever have. I though we were going to die.

When the rumbling stopped, I could hear the condo's fire alarm screaming, making it hard to hear if anyone was hurt and in need of help. When I reached the living room to check my roommate, it seemed there was smoke in the room. I turned to look where our neighbors' condo had been. Through the dim light, I realized their condo had completely collapsed and taken part of ours with it. The smoke I thought I saw was actually drywall dust.

I was terrified because I thought my neighbors were crushed. I shouted their names over and over. My roommate, boyfriend, and I began to scramble to get out of our home but the door was blocked by a staircase which had collapsed. We squeezed through the stone steps and metal rails, walking barefoot over broken glass and fallen bricks.

Our neighbors from the collapsed units were squeezing their way out. We hugged and attempted to comfort one another, saying everything was going to be OK, but we knew we had to get out of the complex.

Like everyone else, we were barefoot and wearing only whatever we had slept in, which in some cases wasn't much. We decided to return to our condo to grab shoes, pants and jackets, but everything was turned upside down in the living room and we couldn't find any flashlights in the darkness.

By the time we got out again, we realized that the people who lived in the condo upstairs were trapped. Their doors were jammed, which actually proved to be a blessing in disguise—the upstairs walkways and railings were all severely damaged or completely destroyed and they might have fallen to their deaths, had they stepped into the darkness. As they began to break open their doors, we yelled to them not to step out. With the help of our flashlights, we got everyone down by passing them from person to person.

I heard someone call my name and when I looked I saw my boyfriend running toward me with a small child in his arms. He shouted, "Take this boy! I don't know who he is!"

We got everyone out and although there were some serious injuries, everyone in the complex survived. Thank goodness.

Not only did January 17th change who I am and where I live, it changed daily habits. I now have emergency lighting throughout my home, flashlights attached to furniture, clothes ready to be slipped into next to my bed and a suitcase packed by the door. Am I overreacting? I don't think so. Now, I'm just prepared.

Sandy Kipp
Professional Musician

Sunday is the day I usually run all my errands. It is the day I get gas for my car, do all my grocery shopping, and banking. But because this was going to be a 3 day weekend and I wanted to take it easy, I decided to put those things off until Monday. That turned out to be a mistake.

I'm a student and I was living in an apartment building across the street from California State University, Northridge. Since I was born and raised in Sacramento and had never experienced an earthquake, I had never learned the precautions one should take.

When the earthquake struck, I thought I was having a nightmare. It sounded like ten locomotives were plowing through my room. When I finally found my flashlight I was shocked to see that everything in my bedroom was in the middle of the floor. After my roommate and I assessed the damage in our rooms, we moved to the kitchen where we found the same situation. This was when I realized that, because of my laziness, I was left with virtually no food, an empty gas tank, and only ten dollars in my pocket.
After I had convinced myself that everything would be fine, my roommate and I decided to see if the earthquake had damaged our cars. The front door of our apartment was jammed shut. We tried to force it open, but to no avail. Fortunately for us, a few minutes later a sizable aftershock managed somehow to un-jam the door.

Our cars were okay, but because the needle on my gas gauge was on empty and all the gas stations in the area were without electricity, my roommate's father drove in from Thousand Oaks to bring me five gallons of gas to get me and my car out of the Valley.

Carey Christensen
College Student

The following is from an interview *conducted with Cathie Woods and Chuck Foerster, residents of a mobile home park located at the very epicenter of the January 17th Northridge Earthquake.*

The mobile home park contains 168 units, mostly single units, but with a few double-wides. Two units caught fire about 15-20 minutes after the earthquake and they in turn, ignited another. Because of broken pipes, there was no water available. The Fire Department sent in a helicopter which made one successful drop, but nearby electric wires made it unsafe for the chopper to return. One fire truck showed up immediately, then moved on, leaving 3 firemen behind to pull down the burning units and keep the fires from spreading.

The fires were apparently caused by gas lines that ruptured when the mobile units were knocked from their piers. Not one trailer in the park came through the earthquake undamaged and only 3 of the 168 units remained on their piers. (One of those had bracing; the other had brick work around it, which helped stabilize it.) Most of the trailers fell away from their porches, which then blocked the exit doors. Other doors were jammed, so residents needed help to exit their homes. Fortunately, only two people were injured and their injuries were minor: an ankle and wrist.

Fire was the residents' first concern. Foerster managed to get out of his home through a window, then joined others going trailer to trailer, turning off the gas. Even so, the smell of leaking gas was still very strong throughout the park because 2 of the 3 main valves at the entrance to the park were leaking.

According to Woods, "The first thing we wanted was a flashlight and there weren't enough to go around. When daylight broke and we were sure there was no leaking gas, we set up our barbecue and began warming tea for ourselves and our neighbors. We immediately began pooling our food reserves, first using food from our freezers and then canned goods. We knew we had enough food to last a few days, but we were unsure about after that. Fortunately, friends drove in from Yucaipa with 2 big barrels of drinking water, water for cleaning, a generator, food, bread, cheese. It was a feeling that 'We're not alone.'"

When the trailers fell, sewage lines were broken so residents couldn't use their toilets. Fortunately, someone in the park suggested placing plastic bags inside toilet bowls, then depositing the sealed bags in the park's waste containers. The Woods family was in somewhat better shape than others. They had a plumber rig a temporary fix on their sewer line so they could at least flush liquids with pool water, then opened their home to others whose homes had been destroyed. According to Woods, "We designated our two bathrooms 'Men's' and 'Women's', gave each person a towel and laid out sleeping bags at night."

The first night, many people either slept on their lawns or in their cars. Concerned about looting were somewhat alleviated by the regular patrols made every 15 minutes by the Los Angeles Police Department.

The 2nd day following the earthquake, large trash barrels and about 20 portable toilets arrived. At last, residents could clear their houses of earthquake debris! To be able to take this admittedly small step was comforting, according to Woods—something they could do to bring some semblance of order to homes which were still sitting all "cockeyed or completely down on the ground."

Many felt they couldn't leave the park because they had to be available for adjusters, contractors and insurance people. So, they sat in front of their wrecked houses all day, waiting. On the third day, they were overjoyed by the arrival of hot meals, provided by the American Red Cross. According to Foerster, "Many residents were totally dependent upon the Red Cross, because there were no stores, no supermarkets and no restaurants open for miles around."

Still, with the passing of each day, an increasing number of residents felt they couldn't continue coping with the situation. Those who could, fled—some to the homes of relatives, others to local motels. Some of the latter then offered to share the comfort of their new-found beds and baths with friends who had stayed behind.

Foerster was one of those who moved out of the park. After his insurance company opened a temporary office in a truck [about 5 miles away] and began handing out checks for living expenses to their insureds, he checked into a motel. As he said, "I was tired of living with no toilet facilities, no way to bathe, no hot water."

According to Woods, the worst part about not having hot water was that they couldn't do laundry. "You want to stay clean and you don't want laundry lying around. We were hand washing essentials, but we had nowhere to dry them."

As for drinking water, they were actually in good shape, thanks to both the American Red Cross and Budweiser, who brought drinking water to the mobile home park on a regular basis. Private citizens even stopped by with water.

It was about a week before residents were able to begin hiring companies to lift trailers and stabilize them on new piers. And according to Foerster, "Some of the contractors took advantage of residents, both by charging too much and by taking money but not returning to do the work." One fellow on Forester's street was taken twice by two different firms, first for $1,700 and then for $1,500. Worse yet, it was only a week later when rates suddenly doubled for the same work!

It wasn't that the residents were ignorant. They did everything they could, calling state offices to make sure the contractors were properly licensed. But as Foerster said, "It didn't mean they would all fulfill their obligations properly." Yet another company whose license was checked and verified, "came in and signed up about 60% of the residents and there was no end to problems. The units weren't leveled properly and we couldn't get them to come back to fix things. It was terrible."

Unfortunately, many residents were acting in a panic, making them easy prey to dishonest contractors. Not all the problems were related to dishonesty, though. State law requires mobile homes to be placed on new piers, and the nearest ones available were in San Diego. Not only did it take time for contractors to make the trip, but they were in competition for a dwindling supply.

Only after the houses were re-positioned on piers did additional damage appear. The very process of re-positioning a mobile home puts strain its structure. Walls were pulled from ceilings, floors from doors, jamming doors which had been operable. All these problems were fixable, once the homes had been properly leveled, but again, it took time.

Telephone service was restored in 2 or 3 days, but residents were 2 weeks without water and 3 weeks without gas and electricity. As Woods said, "By the 2nd or 3rd week we were beginning to feel like we had lost control. Other people were getting back into their homes, but it seemed that there was nothing happening here." She called both her assemblywoman and her councilman, then finally the mayor's office.

"Still, nothing happened. Finally, I got a call back from the assemblywoman's office saying they would come and 'walk the park' on Saturday, but nobody showed. Mysteriously, we got gas and electricity the next day."

According to both Woods and Foerster, there was tremendous cooperation among the residents. "In fact, 2 or 3 days after things had settled down," said Woods, "we commented on what a shame it was that it took an earthquake to introduce us to one another. People really pitched in and made things work as best they could."

When asked what the residents have done since to protect themselves from the eventuality of another earthquake, Foerster said that almost all the units have been retrofitted and properly braced, this made possible through grants from the state of California and FEMA. Those who had earthquake insurance were, for the most part, fairly compensated. But as Foerster said, "There were a lot of people who didn't have insurance and they are still hurting."

He adds that he had his contractor install an emergency exit beneath his bedroom window. It's 2 feet square and all he has to do in the case of an emergency is "turn the handle and I'm out of there!"

When asked if they now felt unsafe living in a mobile home, Woods replied, "Absolutely not. We're safer than other people! Mobile homes don't collapse. The worst they do is fall off the jacks. Furthermore, you don't have far to go to reach the front door so you can get out fast!"

Cathie Woods,
Pharmacy Technical
Chuck Foerster,
Ret., U.S. Post Office

APPENDIX

Earthquake-Related Products and Services

Audio/Video Materials

"Bolt It Down" [video]
Produced by the I.C.B.O. (International Conference of Building Officials)
7998 Georgetown Road; Suite 900
Indianapolis, IN 46268
(800) 243-5736

California Office of Emergency Services Earthquake Program
(More than 60 videos & slide sets available for loan)
101 Eighth Street; Suite 152
Oakland, CA 94607
(510) 540-2713

"On Fire" [video] (Note: Most earthquake related damage is actually from fires.)
Earthquake Preparedness Society
14525 Valley View Ave.; Suite B
Santa Fe Springs, CA 90670
(310) 921-7557

"Surviving the Big One" [video]
Earthquake Preparedness Society
14525 Valley View Ave.; Suite B
Santa Fe Springs, CA 90670
(310) 921-7557

Video Tapes & Slide Sets of numerous recent international earthquakes are available from:
Earthquake Engineering Research Institute
499 14th St., Suite 320
Oakland, CA 94612
(510) 451-0905

Lafferty and Associates
P.O. Box 1026
La Canada, CA 91012
(818) 952-5483

Computer Print-outs Listing School and Business Needs

Earthquake Preparedness Society (A free service.)
14525 Valley View Ave.; Suite B
Santa Fe Springs, CA 90670
(310) 921-7557

Lectures in Training on Earthquake Preparedness

Earthquake Preparedness Society (A free service.)
14525 Valley View Ave.; Suite B
Santa Fe Springs, CA 90670
(310) 921-7557

SOS Technologies
1910 Olympic Blvd.; Suite 311
Walnut Creek, CA 94596
(510) 934-3322

Books, Manuals, Pamphlets & Journals

"An Ounce of Prevention: Strengthening Your Wood Frame House for Earthquake Safety" [book]
California Office of Emergency Services
101 Eighth Street; Suite 152
Oakland, CA 94607
(510) 540-2713

Building Education Center
812 Page St.
Berkeley, CA 94710
(510) 525-7610

California Office of Emergency Services Earthquake Program
101 Eighth Street; Suite 152
Oakland, CA 94607
(510) 540-2713

Earthquake Engineering Research Institute
(Monographs, Reports, Hazard Reduction Planning Publications)
499 14th St., Suite 320
Oakland, CA 94612
(510) 451-0905

Earthquake Preparedness Society
14525 Valley View Ave.; Suite B
Santa Fe Springs, CA 90670
(310) 921-7557

The Emergency Lifeline
1510 East Edinger; Suite D
Santa Ana, CA 92705
(714) 558-8940

Lafferty and Associates
P.O. Box 1026
La Canada, CA 91012
(818) 952-5483

Peace of Mind In Earthquake Country
Peter I. Yanev
Chronicle Books, 1991
(800) 722-6657

Simpler Life Emergency Provisions
1320 Johnson Drive
City of Industry, CA 91745
(818) 961-8858

The Household Inventory Guide
(For taking stock in case of *any* emergency)
Carol Phillips
IPP Press
Post Office Box 8335
Emeryville, CA 94662

Family/Employee Preparedness Training and Hand-books

American Red Cross
2700 Wilshire Blvd.
Los Angeles, CA 90057
(213) 739-5200

Building Education Center
812 Page St.
Berkeley, CA 94710
(510) 525-7610

Earthquake Preparedness Society
14525 Valley View Ave.; Suite B
Santa Fe Springs, CA 90670
(310) 921-7557

Lafferty and Associates
P.O. Box 1026
La Canada, CA 91012
(818) 952-5483

Sands Associates
521 Mill Pond Dr.
San Jose, CA 95125
(408) 288-5700

SOS Technologies
1910 Olympic Blvd.; Suite 311
Walnut Creek, CA 94596
(510) 934-3322

Medical Kits, Water Storage Barrels, Packs, Etc.

Note: Consumable products available from suppliers listed in this section are intended to have a reasonable shelf life and that shelf life should not be near its expiration date when your order is delivered. Check your order carefully and notify the supplier in the event irregularities occur.

American Innotek, Inc.
(Manufacturers kits for the disposal of human wastes)
1565 Creek Street, Ste. 108
San Marcos, CA 92069
(916) 784-0133

CEPP Corporation
2801 E. 12th St.
Los Angeles, CA 90023
(213) 269-9704

Container-Care International
(Storage containers)
P.O. Box 1617
Wilmington, CA 90748
(310) 513-6101

Earthquake Preparedness Society
14525 Valley View Ave.; Suite B
Santa Fe Springs, CA 90670
(310) 921-7557

Extend-A-Life, Inc.
1010 S. Arroyo Pky. #7
Pasadena, CA 91105
(818) 441-1223

The Emergency Lifeline
1510 East Edinger; Suite D
Santa Ana, CA 92705
(714) 558-8940

Property Guard International
6201 Valley Circle Blvd., Ste. 2
Woodland Hills, CA 91367
(800) 703-4660

Sands Associates
521 Mill Pond Dr.
San Jose, CA 95125
(408) 288-5700

Simpler Life Emergency Provisions
1320 Johnson Drive
City of Industry, CA 91745
(818) 961-8858

SOS Technologies
1910 Olympic Blvd.; Suite 311
Walnut Creek, CA 94596
(510) 934-3322

Survivor Industries, Inc.
    2551 Azurite Circle
    Newbury Park, CA 91320
    (805) 498-6062; Fax: (805) 499-3708

Emergency Food and Water Supplies
Note: Consumable products available from suppliers listed in this section are intended to have a reasonable shelf life and that shelf life should not be near its expiration date when your order is delivered. Check your order carefully and notify the supplier in the event irregularities occur.

CEPP Corporation
    2801 E. 12th St.
    Los Angeles, CA 90023
    (213) 269-9704

Earthquake Preparedness Society
    14525 Valley View Ave.; Suite B
    Santa Fe Springs, CA 90670
    (310) 921-7557

The Emergency Lifeline
    1510 East Edinger; Suite D
    Santa Ana, CA 92705
    (714) 558-8940

Extend-A-Life, Inc.
    1010 S. Arroyo Pky. #7
    Pasadena, CA 91105
    (818) 441-1223

FR & Assoc., Inc.
    124 Parker Ave.
    Rodeo, CA 94572
    (800) 854-4905

Marin Outdoors
    49 Simms Street
    San Rafael, CA 94901
    (415) 453-3400

Pro-Motion Ltd.
    1723 E. Portner
    West Covina, CA 91791
    (818) 919-5700

Property Guard International
    (Can manufacture Kosher survival food in large quantities.)
    6201 Valley Circle Blvd., Ste. 2
    Woodland Hills, CA 91367
    (800) 703-4660

Ready Reserve Foods
P.O. Box 697
Beaumont, CA 92223
(909) 796-0098

Sands Associates
521 Mill Pond Dr.
San Jose, CA 95125
(408) 288-5700

Simpler Life Emergency Provisions
1320 Johnson Drive
City of Industry, CA 91745
(818) 961-8858

Sam Andy Foods
1442 South Gage St.
San Bernardino, CA 92408
(909) 796-4777

SOS Survival Life Support
N. 3808 Sullivan Rd., Bldg. #6
Spokane, WA 99216
(206) 726-9363

SOS Technologies
1910 Olympic Blvd.; Suite 311
Walnut Creek, CA 94596
(510) 934-3322

Survival, Inc.
2633 Eastlake Ave. E., Ste. 103
Seattle, WA 98102
(206) 726-9363, (800) 292-4707

Survivor Industries, Inc.
2551 Azurite Circle
Newbury Park, CA 91320
(805) 498-6062; Fax: (805) 499-3708

Miscellaneous Products & Services

Conservation Materials, Ltd.™
1395 Greg St., Ste. #110
Sparks, NV 89431
(800) 733-5283

Earthquake Preparedness Society
14525 Valley View Ave.; Suite B
Santa Fe Springs, CA 90670
(310) 921-7557

Fastening Solutions
(Non-structural safety fasteners)
15230 Burbank Blvd., Suite 106
Van Nuys, CA 91411
(818) 994-6398; Fax (818) 997-1371

National Earthquake Information Center
   (Up-to-date information regarding earthquakes worldwide. Monthly updates published for subscribers. Also seismicity maps.)
   U. S. Department of the Interior
   Geological Survey
   M.S. 967
   Box 25046 Federal Center
   Denver, CO 80225
   (303) 273-8516 (For recorded information on worldwide earthquake actity during preceding 24 hours.), (303) 273-8500 (To speak with personnel, 7:30 a.m.-4:30 p.m. MDT. Then voice mail answers.)

Pyramid
   (Manufacturers portable cooking systems which use multiple types of fuel.)
   3292 S. Highway 97
   Redmond, OR 97756
   (800) 824-4288

Q-Safety, Inc.
   (Earthquake stabilization & safety products for inside the home.)
   2335 East Foothill Blvd.
   Pasadena, CA 91107
   (818) 449-1590; (800) 997-2338

Quake Hold Fastening Products, Inc.™
   129 East Colorado Blvd.; Ste. 462
   Monrovia, CA 91016
   (818) 301-0891; (800) 418-7348

Skyboy Sales
   (Diesel powered fire fighting pump/8k generator.)
   7152 Sunset Blvd.
   Hollywood, CA 90046
   (213) 874-6454

Strand Earthquake Consultants
   (Seismic actuators, seismic switches, seismographs, educational programs, preparedness consulting.)
   1436 South Bentley Avenue #6
   Los Angeles, CA 90025
   (800) 978-7263, (310) 473-2316

Trevco
   (Fastening devices for furniture, electronics & appliances)
   129 East Colorado Blvd., Ste. 462
   Monrovia, CA 91016
   (818) 301-0891; (800) 418-7348

WorkSafe Technologies™
   (Seismic & environmental safety products & services.)
   25133 Avenue Tibbitts, Bldg. F
   Valencia, CA 91355
   (805) 257-2527

Glass - Safety Film Coating

Armorcoat
(Safety and Security Film for Windows)
1045 South Bixel St. 2nd Fl.
Los Angeles, CA 90015
(213) 747-1391

Endur-All Glass Coatings, Inc.
(Safety and Security Film for Existing Flatt Glass)
P.O. Box 3453
Granada Hills, CA 91394-0453
(818) 366-3437

Quake Proof, Inc.
2339 3rd St., Ste. 34
San Francisco, CA 94107
(415) 863-0511

Sunmaster
47 Quail Ct., Ste. 106
Walnut Creek, CA 94596
(916) 568-0005

Window Solutions, Inc.
(Safety and Security Film for Windows)
1169 Chess Drive, Suite K
Foster City, CA 94404
(800) 782-0660

Gas Shut-off Valves (Automatic)

See chapter entitled *AUTOMATIC GAS SHUT-OFF VALVES* for full listing of all licensed manufacturers

Gas Shut-off Wrenches

Earthquake Preparedness Society
14525 Valley View Ave.; Suite B
Santa Fe Springs, CA 90670
(310) 921-7557

Property Guard International
6201 Valley Circle Blvd., Ste. 2
Woodland Hills, CA 91367
(800) 703-4660

Roy Pollard Co.
27703-14 Ortega Hwy.
San Juan Capistrano, CA   92675
(714) 661-1988

Simpler Life Emergency Provisions
1320 Johnson Drive
City of Industry, CA 91745
(818) 961-8858

Additional Sources of Earthquake-Related Information

California Office of Emergency Services Earthquake Program
    101 Eighth Street; Suite 152
    Oakland, CA 94607
    (510) 540-2713

Business and Industry Council for Emergency Planning and Preparedness
    2700 Wilshire Blvd.
    Los Angeles, CA 90057
    (213) 386-4524

California Division of Mines and Geology
    107 South Broadway; Room 1065
    Los Angeles, CA 90012
    (213) 620-3560
    (Available: Geologic information, publication sales, referrals, study zonation maps for some areas for reference only.)

California Division of Mines and Geology
    Publications
    801 K Street; MS14-33
    Sacramento, CA 95814-3531
    (916) 445-5716
    (Available: Geologic information, publication sales, referrals, study zonation maps. Geologist on duty.)

California Division of Mines and Geology
    185 Berry Street., Ste. 3600
    San Francisco, CA 94107
    (415) 904-7707
    (Available: Geologic information, publication sales, referrals, study zonation maps for some areas.)

California Institute of Technology
    1201 East California Blvd.
    Pasadena, CA 91125
    Public Information Office: (818) 395-3003 (For general earthquake information.)
    Hot Line: (818) 395-6977 (For specific information regarding earthquakes in previous 24 hours.)

California Seismic Safety Commission
    1900 K Street; Suite 100
    Sacramento, CA 95814
    (916) 322-4917
    (An Advisory Commission. Available: "California at Risk; Reducing Earthquake Hazards"– a book listing agencies which deal with earthquake related issues and concerns. Also: "Homeowners' Guide To Earthquake Safety" and "The Commercial Property Owners' Guide to Earthquake Safety." Various publications dealing with virtually all aspects of earthquake related issues.)

Earthquake Preparedness Society
    14525 Valley View Ave.; Suite B
    Santa Fe Springs, CA 90670
    (310) 921-7557

Earth Science Information Center
    A Division of the U.S. Geological Survey
    (800) 872-6277
    (Available: Maps)

Earthquake Engineering Research Institute
499 14th St., Suite 320
Oakland, CA 94612-1934
(510) 451-0905
(Multi-disciplinary organization. Papers by researchers & practitioners dedicated to earthquake hazard reduction.)

Federal Emergency Management Agency (FEMA)
Region 9; Building 105
Presidio of San Francisco
San Francisco, CA 94129
(800) 525-0321
(Available: More than 80 publications in their "Earthquake Hazards Reduction Series"; maps.)

General Disaster Information:
State Office of Emergency Services
Public Affairs
2800 Meadowview Road
Sacramento, CA 95832
Ph. (916) 262-1843
(Earthquake preparedness kits containing brochures, check-list, etc. Information regarding structural retrofitting, preparedness for the disabled, FEMA, etc.)

Governor's Office of Emergency Services
1110 East Green Street, Suite 300
Pasadena, CA 91106
Ph. (818) 304-8383   (For organizations seeking assistance with earthquake preparedness.)
HOT LINE: (800) 286-7233 (Info. available in multiple languages. "How to" prepare homes, schools, etc. Special information for disabled and seniors.)

Office of Emergency Services
1350 Front Street; Suite 4015
San Diego, CA 92101
(619) 525-4287

S.E.A.O.N.C. - Northern California Office
50 First Street, Suite #300
San Francisco, CA 94105
(415) 974-5147

S.E.A.O.C.C. - Central California Office
P.O. Box 2590
Fair Oaks, CA 95628
(916) 965-1536

S.E.A.O.S.D. - San Diego Office
P.O. Box 26500, Suite #203
San Diego, CA 92126
(619) 223-9955

S.E.A.O.S.C. - Southern California Office
5360 South Workman Mill Road
Whittier, CA 90601
(310) 908-6131

S.E.A.O.C. - State of California
1050 Fulton Ave. #150
Sacramento, CA 95825
(916) 427-3647

State Office of Emergency Services Resource Center
    117 West Micheltorena; Suite D
    Santa Barbara, CA 93101
    (805) 568-1209
    (Available: Information for elderly, disabled, pre-schools, apartment dwellers, etc. Also a loan-out video library)

U.S. Geological Survey
    Earth Science Info. Center, Building 3
    MS-532
    345 Middlefield Rd.
    Menlo Park, CA 94025
    (415) 329-4390
    (Available: Seismic maps, general geologic information, aerial photographs, satellite data.)

Stores Specializing in Earthquake Preparedness

Note: The following stores for the most part, do not manufacturer products. But because they tend to stock a wide variety of products made by manufacturers listed elsewhere in the Appendix, they are a rich resource for one-stop shopping.

Disaster Preparedness
    1405 El Camino Real,Suite 110
    Oceanside, CA 92054
    (800) 800-7922, (619) 966-3600

Earthquake Outlet
    981 San Pablo Ave.
    Albany, CA 94706
    (510) 526-3587

Earthquake Outlet
    2225 Broadway
    Redwood City, CA 94063
    (415) 368-8800

Earthquake Services and Products
    31143 Villa Colina #502
    Westlake Village, CA
    (800) 889-5220; (800) 377-8888

Parkin Security Consultants
    7758 Bark Lane
    San Jose, CA 95129
    (408) 255-4564

INDEX

NOTES

ORDER BLANK

Please send me:

_____ copies of **EARTHQUAKE PREPARED** @ $10.95 per copy   _____

    California residents add 8.25% tax   _____

    Postage & handling for one copy   <u>   1.50 </u>

    Postage & handling for *additional* copies @ 50¢ each   _____

                               TOTAL ENCLOSED   _____

My Name_____

Address:_____

City_____State_____Zip_____

Make checks payable to:

Studio 4 Productions

Post Office Box 280400
Northridge, CA 91328-0400